# THE SHATTERED FAÇADE

## REBEKAH MOWBRAY

Published by the Power Writers Publishing Group in 2021.

 A catalogue record for this book is available from the National Library of Australia

NATIONAL LIBRARY OF AUSTRALIA

ISBN: 978-0-6452120-0-6 (pbk)
ISBN: 978-0-6452120-1-3 (ebk)

Cover by Samantha Nagle copyright 2021.

Typesetting by Publicious Book Publishing
www.publicious.com.au

**Disclaimer**
Any opinions expressed in this work are exclusively those of the author and are not necessarily the views held or endorsed by others quoted throughout. All of the information, and concepts contained within the publication are intended for general information only. The author does not take any responsibility for any choices that any individual or organization may make with this information in the business, personal, financial, familial or other areas of life.

*To my family,*
*The pillar in my unrelenting storm,*
*I thank and honour you.*
*You have sacrificed.*
*You have loved.*
*You never let me go.*

# TABLE OF CONTENTS

# ABOUT THE AUTHOR

Rebekah Anne Mowbray is a spirit-led woman grounded in the Australian creative and social services industry. With credits in award-winning films, she is a talented Federation University trained actress, classically trained singer, composer, poet and pianist.

Known for crafting emotive poems in less time than it would take to butter toast, Rebekah is a deeply engaging storyteller – delighting both her elderly clients and youthful friends – with an amalgamation of past and present stories that would ordinarily encompass many lifetimes.

From abuse, near-death experiences abroad, and having her wedding cancelled only hours before the planned date, Rebekah is known for telling stories of 'dark' moments with a smile and understanding grace.

With a passion to live with authentic resilience, Rebekah is committed to reminding others that hope can blossom in the most trying of circumstances – even when there's many reasons to give up.

———ⲟⲉⲋⲟ———

# PROLOGUE

For years I wore a façade. Riddled with pain and addiction, I was the living definition of the word 'hypocrite.'

Christian living isn't always easy, especially if you're existing in the midst of a storm. I needed to find 'order' within the 'disorder.' I needed to face the tornado of chaos and step into its eye.

God told me to write about walking through life with a mindset of 'from victory, into victory' – even when you don't feel victorious. This was a concept I had never fully grasped but knew I had to embrace. I didn't know if I had the courage to ride the storm. I didn't know if I'd glean the keys and obtain victory. But I knew I had to try.

If I wanted to have an abundant life like the scriptures said, I would have to stop hiding from the wind and waves. I would have to put a stake in the ground and dig my roots deep! It was time to face the demon in my mind: **me**.

This book is 'faith in action.' I am believing I will see my victory as I write from it. I have had to shatter the old reflection of myself to see the truth – the warrior in waiting, the conqueror in hiding.

May *The Shattered Façade* be a token of hope. Whether you're in a battle, or know someone who is fighting, **you**

**are not alone**. I pray that as you glance into my reality, shackles of shame will break off, scales on eyes will fall and strongholds will shatter. God is greater than any and every demon you might face and so are you.

It's time to meet the victor in hiding, the conqueror within.

God said:

*"You are more than a conqueror."*
*But what does that mean?*
*The meaning seems so hard to perceive.*
*Simplistic in view,*
*simplistic in sound,*
*the Lord of all does resound:*

*YOU ARE MORE THAN A CONQUEROR!*

I knew the meaning, but the reality of walking in and from freedom was foreign. I didn't know what it was like to have a warrior mentality as a worrier, or to have a victor mentality as a victim. I had to learn to live a life with a spirit of abundance – living rather than just existing.

I knew what He said but the monumental mountain, the thorn in my side, it never seemed to dissipate. It continued to reside! No matter how hard I'd try it would remain. No matter how far I'd run and hide it would still find me, follow me and gnaw at me day and night, night and day.

He said, "I AM MORE THAN A CONQUEROR."

Why didn't my life reflect that?

Was it because I had not grasped how much bigger He was – how much grander, greater, stronger and smarter? Was it because I hadn't soaked in His presence enough, or that my eyes hadn't truly gleaned the treasures of His words? That I had not fully perceived the wisdom inside? What was it? I didn't understand why my suffering remained.

I have since come to realise that answers lie in my willingness to align with His promises.

In these words and songs of life, love, loss and me, I voice my struggle. Likewise, I reveal the inner recalibration that comes with standing on His truth. I may not have reached my destination yet, but I proclaim that **I will be** all that He says I am. I will not give up. I will persevere and I will be transformed from glory to glory.

He has script my life. I just need to read, apply and live out as He guides.

And I will.

For **I am** *more* than a conqueror and my friend, **you are too!**

# Poisoned

*I grew up with the most beautiful family.*
*I have the most beautiful family,*
*but somehow poison seeped through the cracks.*

Kim and Kay lived south of Sydney with three beautiful girls, each a year apart. Kim's family lived in Victoria, Kay's in Queensland. Somehow, this family of five found themselves sandwiched in between.

One year would roll into the next and like any other 'normal' family, there were hiccups and mishaps every now and again. But all in all, it was a home of love, laughter and of course sibling rivalry.

There were daily strolls, scheduled naps, play dates, hearty home-cooked meals and Sunday mornings at church. This was a picture perfect family.

Every year they would travel north or south to one side of the extended family. This particular year they would drive into the land of humidity and heat.

The holiday season had begun.

With three little girls bundled up in the back of their car, Kim and Kay started their annual drive. The backseat was an image of planned chaos. Together with stuffed animals, pillows and blankets, they travelled into the dead of night. Hours passed. Kim and Kay tag teamed driving and sleeping as night turned into day. Another night, another day and finally, *finally* after many games of 'I spy...' and many a wet eye, they pulled into Grandma's driveway.

Aunts and uncles filled the house, cousins bustling in and out. The house hummed. Although they thought it was safe, although we all thought it was safe, there was a wolf in the flock.

None would foresee the future that was about to unfold.

Nothing would ever be the same.

Innocence was lost.

Once.

Twice.

A fairytale ended. Reality began.

Poison had infected a little heart, a tiny mind, a meek body and birthed a wounded spirit.

# Fiery Little Tacker

Before all this took place, I was a fiery little tacker.

I loved music and dance. I thought everyone could sing, that it was nothing special. I would stand in front of the mirror, wrap a towel around my shoulders like a cape and strut up and down the hallway.

> This four-year-old had style
> and perhaps an extra spoonful of spunk!

Every night the three sisters would huddle around their mother. Bible stories would be read and together they'd say their prayers before brushing their teeth and getting tucked up in bed.

The youngest daughter knew God existed – the stories were proof enough. From Abraham to Isaac, from Daniel to David, it was all common facts to this little four-year-old.

One day, she got her hands on a small red New Testament Bible. That evening after story-time she secretly pulled it out from under her pillow. Frustrated that her tiny life wasn't very adventurous and that she couldn't read all the fine print – but knowing it contained the stories her mother told – she prayed a big, adventurous prayer:

"God, if you exist, I want Jesus to come back to earth. There needs to be a *new* New Testament – I want to be in it! All these people seemed normal at the beginning and then got to be in these stories... I'm normal, make me special too!"

What a handful her folks had.

At preschool waiting to be picked up, a mother approached her and asked, "Honey, what do you want to be when you're a grown up?"

"I'm going to be a star –
not one in the sky, one on the stage!"

Yup, her folks certainly **did** have a lot on their hands!

It's extraordinary looking back. An innocent young life was so radically distorted by a simple holiday. The once vivacious little girl now hid a secret seed.

Weeds festered in the dark unbeknownst to everyone else.

Years later, those weeds crept into the light.

It seemed unfathomable.

My parents had followed 'the book' to a tee. They loved greatly and they protected in every way they knew how. They trusted, but that trust was abused – on multiple occasions.

I beg to question, who is safe?

It's staggering to see the impact abuse had on us.

Looking now at the relationships and side effects, the pain of all... it's evident that wounded soldiers fight and cope very differently.

At the end of the day it was not just one wounded heart, but five.

Abuse shatters.

# Time Was Not Kind

Time was not kind to my little mind, nor was society to my tender heart.

By the time primary school neared a close and schoolyard bullies moved to new yards, the damage had already been done.

High school started and before the year ended, Grandma passed. The seed of death manifested.

Life was no longer desired.

Finding it hard to make friends, I would perform, be seen and then judged.

After a nasty comment from a young performer and her mother – hyper-vigilant about body image – I became obsessed with my weight.

I started to lose a little. People started to notice and comment.

"You look so good!"
*(So this is how you make friends?)*

Before I could blink, I was in the snare of a vicious eating disorder. I was in a death trap.

# The Death Trap

Another hole to be punched on the old belt. Nothing fit, yet still I wasn't content. My days of laughter and joy had turned hazy and dull – I was a living corpse.

The monotonous nightmare continued, day in and day out. If the numbers were happy, I'd be spared the 4am workout, but it was never enough for breakfast or lunch...

Walking to school lugging a heavy bag of textbooks, I was in constant competition with the cars – who would make it to the telegraph pole first?

This unrealistic goal was just another means to reiterate the failure I felt I was.

*See, you failed* **again**! *Put your head down, you don't deserve to be seen.*

I'd stand behind the classrooms.

Dammit! I'm ten minutes early. They're all staring at me... should I try to talk to them?

*And be laughed at? No way!*

Maybe I should walk to the bathroom? It's on the other side of the school and people won't stare as much.

*Yes, that's a good idea. Just remember, make the most out of it – you'll be sitting for a whole two hours!*

"Rebekah, your results."

Failed again! You know what that means.

"Why is your page blank?"

"I've been thinking, Miss..."

"... *too* much in my view!
What are you doing to yourself?
You're turning into nothing!"

Argh! Not in front of the popular kids. Just what I want – more bitching about me.

"Why don't you have any recess snacks?"

"Oh, well... I was running a little late and forgot. I'm not really hungry though."

The rest of the day would be a blur until the dreaded time I'd arrive home.

What am I going to do when I get home?

I mustn't go near the kitchen or food...

*Hide in the laundry, go on the computer, research 'Me,' just don't let anyone see you. Remember to delete the computer history. They mustn't find out!*

"Rebekah! It's dinner time."

Please don't find me, Mum.

"Rebekah, you've got one more chance!"

"I had some dinner earlier Mum and I've got so much homework to do."

"Come on, let's eat as a family."

*GO! Your family is waiting.*

"That's it, Rebekah! I know you haven't had anything. **Come down now!**"

Panic boiled in my veins. I willed my feet to the kitchen.

Gah, relief at last.

"Mum, I told you I was right about Rebekah! Look what's in the toilet!"

Oh my God, I've got to hide.
How could I forget? What should I do?

"Rebekah, that's the last straw. You're going to the doctors. They're expecting us, get in the car!"

"No, no, NO, **NO! I won't! You can't make me! I don't care that I'm acting like a child! I'm not going!**"

Uncontrollable frustration erupted from my being. They didn't understand. They didn't know what this meant. I couldn't go. I mustn't. The consequences...

Wishing, hoping and praying I could remain in ignorance, my being was suddenly forced into reality. I could no longer control it.

"Fine. Kim, pick her up. I'll go to the front, you go to the back."

**"Get off me! This is abuse! Don't, please. I'll be good. Please. No. NO!"**

Tears cascaded down my face but they meant nothing. Dad hauled me over his shoulders. The beast within raged. Biting as hard as I could, blood started to ooze down his arm.

Please Mum, no. Let me be. Love me like you love my sisters...

*Overcast clouds gathered around the crown of my head as wave upon wave of chilling emptiness battered me in its seas.*

"Haha... yes, it's a funny story. You see, the reason we don't have a door handle on the bathroom is it's the only room in the house with a lock and, well, our daughter would lock herself in there for hours at a time."

"Rebekah, come out of the bathroom and have lunch, please."

**"Rebekah, come out of that darn bathroom and have some lunch!** Not again... what am I going to do with that girl?"

I can't do this anymore. All day, every day – I'm locked in this prison of hell. I can't escape. There's no way out and **they're making me fat!** I need to get out of here!

Maybe I should start sneaking showers again after meals. Or I know, I'll smuggle a container into my room. They won't notice...

**My voice.** My precious voice.

Gone...

The one thing that defined me, that gave me hope. Strength. Purpose.

Ruined...

No longer could I escape with the delicate gift of music. No longer could I talk from dawn to dusk. No longer could I escape the webbed nightmare.

*Trapped.*

*Life stripped me bare,*
*I was shattered.*

"Rebekah, where are you? We need to leave in the next five minutes!"

She won't find me if I'm silent, hidden in a ball behind the tattered lounge, cobwebs clinging to my arms. The repulsion. The clinging webs mirrored my suffocating inner turmoil.

Reality whipped me in its stride.

Thoughts quickly dismissed.

Footsteps came closer...

"We need to leave now or we'll be late! Rebekah, stop fooling around. I don't have time for your crap this morning!"

I can't believe she thinks I'll just go... especially after they **promised** not to take me away – to send me to that place. NO, I'LL NOT GO! She won't find me. She can't...

Please don't let her find me.

"Kim, would you help me? We were supposed to leave ten minutes ago and I still don't know where that girl is!'

"Kay, where are you? **I've found her Kay! Kay?"**

*Quick, you don't have much time. Run! Hide again!* **You mustn't go today!** *You see what they've done to Kate. DON'T let that happen to you as well. Sarah's cupboard,* *your Mum's already checked there. She won't look again for a while.* **RUN! GO!**

My heart raced. I ran on the icy slate as quietly as possible. **Hurry**!

"Okay, she's in the kitchen. We can leave now."

**"Rebekah! Why the hell aren't you in the kitchen? Get out here now! We're twenty five minutes late!"**

Cramped inside a small cupboard one foot squashed an old shoebox. Boney arms attempted to brace my body. The discomfort was more than apparent. Not wanting to cause any damage but needing to stay unseen, a new battle took forth – the battle to breathe.

My heart felt like it would beat right out of my chest. I swore its palpitations could be heard.

Attempting to breathe more silently, the battle within my body began to rage. Wanting to gasp for air to gulp it down, sips were only permitted. It wasn't enough to satisfy my exhausted body, but I had to keep silent. I couldn't be found. My head started to spin like an uncontrollable carousel.

I had to get it together.

Blinking to retain consciousness, I peered through the tiny opening of the door.

Dark shadows flickered past.

I watched...

I waited...

Crying inside, I attempted to calm myself. Boiling anger seethed through my veins, through my hands. They began to shake.

*You must stop. You must stay calm. They'll hear the rattling cupboard!*

But I'm so tired.

*NO, YOU AREN'T! Don't give up... you know how much I like it when you **give up!***

The deeply embedded seed of hate grew inside my being. Glaring into the nauseating scenery and watching, it sped by.

They'd promised.

Mum, stop doing that. Stop doing that. STOP DOING THAT! Don't you realise what writing those numbers down does to me? Every week! Everyone can see them in the book. I hear you telling my sisters, I hear you telling our relatives and your friends. Stop it. STOP IT!

"I can't believe you're doing this to our family. Mum and Dad have never fought until now. They'll probably get a divorce because of you. You're a selfish b\*\*tch. Just f\*\*kin' eat! It's not that hard!"

I am nothing.

No-one.

It's hard to believe that wasn't just a small chapter of my life but a large reality of my adolescence.

Memories of my sisters at home are scarce. The rare moments I can account for my eldest sister, Naomi, are when she'd be in a yelling fit with me, only to disappear shortly after.

It has taken her **many** years to forgive me. The pain I caused during that long season was extraordinary and it heightened the pain already present.

They were very long years of suffering for everyone.

Sarah, my other sister, responded differently. I remember her sitting with me at the kitchen table helping me consume an insufferably small amount of food. Mum would have had enough, Dad could never help, but Sarah had a special way.

My mind would create these monstrous barricades, surrounding me, suffocating me. Unbearable darkness would engulf me sometimes slowly, at other times it would plague my consciousness. I was trapped.

Sarah didn't judge but... understood.

I remember she'd let me borrow her clothes as mine slowly constricted around my waist. I was so self-conscious and caged myself in our place of residence. It was no longer at home but in prison... our prison.

Visitors rarely came within close proximity of our house – my agonising wails deterred them.

I remember going to the front of the church time and time again for healing, for breakthrough, for peace. After a while, I heard whispers from others in the pews.

Little niggles.

"She's up there again..."
"I bet she'll cry too."
"Wanna make a bet she'll be up there next week as well?"

Humiliated.

Ashamed.

Scared.

Exhausted.

Nowhere was safe.

So much for the God of the Bible.

# Like a Vapour

*Faith disappeared like a vapour.*

Life turned into a shadow. I'd turned into a shadow. Taken out of school I was home-schooled and chaperoned to multiple weekly specialists. I wasn't to be trusted.

The following year I was locked up in a ward.

Eventually I returned to school, however, there was a catch – I would graduate behind my peers. Socially there were obstacles. There always was. I never fully fit in and now being in the year below, it was even harder.

Head down, persevere.

A teacher pulled me aside after I returned, after I'd successfully graduated from Refeeding School.

She was my drama teacher:

"Rebekah, thank you very much. You've made me terrified for my daughter. You looked like the ghost of death when you left. Now, I'm constantly terrified that could happen to her."

"Ummm... sorry Miss... I'm sure it won't..."

—— ✺ ——

*You cannot hide from the woman inside.*

—— ✺ ——

School eventually ended, but despair and inner pain were constant friends.

A fierce jealousy would blaze when I'd see my sisters and their friends. However, a deep shame would reign if they invited me to join them. There was this persistent gnawing that something was inherently wrong with me. Why wasn't I loved and accepted for myself?

Sarah had been gallivanting around South America backpacking. Upon my graduation, she emailed me to join her. I was unhappy, she was happy – why not join the adventure?

I had saved enough pennies after working for most of my adolescent days in a nursing home. I could afford it... I just wasn't sure.

I mentioned the idea to Mum and later overheard my eldest sister conversing with her:

"Rebekah's just saying she'll go, but she never will. She doesn't have the gumption."

Rebellion and indignation coursed through my veins. The next day I purchased a one-way ticket.

I'd show them!

A new adventure was about to begin.

# A Step of Faith

With a shaky step and a fear-filled heart, there was a knowing that if I remained in Australia, I would eventually depart. With a hopeful hop, I boarded the plane. Perhaps this journey would lead me somewhere better and I'd get stronger.

For years, I'd fill my mind with self-help wisdom. Whether it was Anthony Robbins or Wayne Dyer, sermons from 'super-pastors,' gurus, neuro linguistic hypnotherapists or the like, I tried hard to find a way to rid myself of the demons within. It was beyond disconcerting to realise just how dark and hopeless life could be and just how empty and numb I'd become when change didn't come.

I was a lifeless life and could only pray this journey would change that reality.

I ran from my world for seven months. After the first two, my sister returned to our homeland.

Then I travelled solo.

# Finding my Feet

Entering a foreign land, the bustle of a new culture, new language and new atmosphere, I didn't know where to look at first. I didn't even know what to feel.

I was beyond exhausted. My sister scooped me up onto a scooter and took me to the most beautiful organic coffee farm to rest.

We stayed with a Colombian family in the mountains. With a house that looked more like a treehouse with no windows, their simplicity of living both charmed and disarmed me.

With no technology, I struggled to lull the busyness in my mind. With no agenda, no deadline and nothing to do, I struggled in silence. I didn't know what to do when life stopped and watching the Amazonian birds, beautiful as they were, stirred a racing within. I didn't know who I was when I wasn't 'doing' and I didn't know how to stop the inner voices.

I didn't know peace.

Time with the family came to a close and my sister and I started travelling to some of the most exquisite sights in all the world. It was extraordinary being so in awe of the beauty and likewise wanting to fade into it. The more we travelled, the more I realised I couldn't run from the demons within. A busy schedule would only keep them at bay for so long. They always returned, louder than before.

As a little girl, I used to dream about living with the Amish. Their simple lifestyle, their love, their humble spirituality and strong community values made me want to belong like nothing else. For years, I'd escape to the scripted world of Beverly Lewis, to Pennsylvania, Ohio, to an Amish county and I'd dwell in that place of peace. There I was safe.

Now, travelling in Bolivia, my sister and I had the opportunity to do just that – live with an Amish family in the Amazon jungle! I would live my fantasy. After an abysmal flight into the jungle and riding in a van that broke down, after being robbed and wading through rivers carrying our packs on top of our heads and later hitching scooters, we arrived unannounced at an Amish family's doorstep.

The unannounced guests were anxious, smelly and sweaty, but were welcomed with open arms.

We arrived just in time for church.

With wooden pews, the transformed kitchen had become a cathedral. The thrice-translated sermon finished three and a half hours later. Exhausted but elated, we had just stepped into another world.

# The Amazonian Amish

With no technology and machetes to clear the farmland, this Amish family had built a waterwheel, house, a few outhouses and a barn by hand. They'd established a Western farm in the middle of the jungle!

> It was as though we'd stepped back in time and
> were living among the pioneers.

Rising early to stoke the fire to bake bread and blowing out the lanterns after the sun raised its head was wonderful, until it wasn't.

This had been my dream. These people weren't supposed to have problems, but problems they had.

> Something deep within my heart became awfully sad.
> My safe place wasn't safe in reality.

My faith was as strong as a strand of string. Could I hope in anything?

One evening, after attempting to cook a lemon meringue pie without an electric beater, I realised it was the one piece of technology I didn't want to have to live without. Perhaps the Amish way of living wasn't for me.

Joe, the father, sat me down and our time of storytelling began. He shared their history and in the midst of his tales told me about another community: the Mennonites. They were very similar to the Amish but embraced some modern conveniences. My ears instantly pricked.

*I could be Mennonite!*

Before I could unpack that fantasy further another voice immediately overrode the first.

*Get that stupid thought out of your head, Rebekah.*
*You're never going to become a Mennonite.*
*You'll never even meet one!*

It was time to part ways. Adventures and stories filled our days. From bungee jumping with frayed ropes to terrifying buses on death-defying roads, to being alone and followed on streets, then being attacked by a gang as they tried to drag us out of the taxi...

*We were stopped in the centre lane. Sandwiched at the traffic lights, there was an alley to our right. It was dark. I saw a gang standing nearby. They watched. They came over.*

*Naively, I thought they were going to ask the driver for directions. They surrounded the taxi – our taxi. My window, slightly ajar, had fingers pressing in. They smashed a window. No, they definitely didn't need directions!*

*Blanketed by glass, Sarah screamed. I looked at the man by my door. I looked in his eyes – they were black.*

*His hate penetrated my soul. The door opened. My door. Playing tug-of-war, he won. He grabbed me by the shoulders. That was it.*

I'm dead!

He was too strong, there were too many men!

*My sister let go of her bag and grabbed onto me. They fought over me. The traffic lights turned green and half out of the car, we sped into the distance... into freedom.*

What a journey!

I can safely say we made some of the most extraordinary memories – snorkelling in the Galápagos Islands, wandering the wonder-filled Machu Picchu ruins, not to mention the magnificent spray from Iguazu Falls – we met so many people, both good and bad, regardless of their circumstances. But happy or sad, the demon within me still taunted. I could never escape that constant agony within. Not even near-death experiences silenced it.

In a season of spiritual unbelief, I ironically witnessed God spare my life time and time again. I'd hear an inner voice tell me what to do when we were robbed, or when I was stranded, penniless and alone on an island, the voice showed me a way out. I saw Him position people on my path when I was positively desperate and I constantly saw the faithfulness of the Voice. It religiously saved me from imminent disaster. Over and over again the Voice came through and I was saved – just.

Still in a state of such sadness, God's efforts to prove His faithfulness seemed futile.

He was too late.

# Eternal Sleep

*Eternal sleep was a constant temptation.*

It wasn't a good day. Beyond desperate and travelling solo, I'd missed yet **another** bus! Tired and weary, I eventually arrived a week late in a picturesque Patagonian village, Bariloche. I was not a happy camper.

In the most glorious of locations, I would berate myself for being so self-absorbed and depressed. Despair plagued me every day.

Weary from the painted façade, frustrated by the futile worldly wisdom I was constantly soaking in, I couldn't hide. I couldn't escape myself, no matter how far I travelled or how hard I tried!

On a day like any other the chains of despair were heavy – too heavy. I was tired of the battle, the torment amidst the most glorious of places. I despised myself.

Not knowing how to change my inner environment, no longer knowing what to do, I planned how to make everything cease.

Hours into planning, my thoughts thick as mud, I got interrupted. A jarring inner voice shook me into reality.

*Rebekah, stop being* **so** *ridiculous! SNAP OUT OF IT!*
*Talk to someone – anyone!*

Obediently, I looked at the woman next to me in the tiny hostel. Taking in a breath and with a rough, raw voice I blurted:

"Hi. What's your name? I'm Bek! What're you doing here?"

"Hi Bek, I'm Jean. I'm a Mennonite missionary."

WHAT?

This was too bizarre to be true! Of all people, she just happened to be Mennonite?

As she shared her story, I learnt she was part of a team – the 'Reach Team.' She shared how they were working in Chile and only came across the border into Argentina for seven days to renew their passports.

*Had I caught my initial bus,*
*I would have missed them.*

A few days passed and as I watched them together, I saw the love – the community. A deep longing rose within my soul.

I wanted to be part of their team.

The hostel manager interrupted my daydreaming. He told me I had to leave immediately. I'd forgotten to reserve another night. They needed my bed. I had to get out. NOW!

Back in a state of hopelessness, not knowing where to go or what to do, I glanced back at the Mennonites. They were laughing, happy.

Internally, I cried out to God.

"God, if you truly exist, prove it! Let me be part of their team, part of their family. It's impossible, of course, because I'm never going to see them again and that's all your fault!"

It was completely irrational and untrue, yet God became my punching bag. I needed someone, or something, to project my disappointment upon.

With daggers of pain, I hurled them at God!

# The Unlikely Encounter

A pair of English sisters spontaneously crossed my path. Meeting in a different hostel, they were like a hot cup of tea and a slice of crusty toast on a cold winter's day. They personified my romantic notion of home.

Anna was the doctor. Prim, proper, strong features and a strong heart – she fascinated me. I'd watch, I'd listen and quietly I'd observe her relationship with her sister, Kate.

Kate was the teacher. Soft around the edges, she had the temperament of a jolly larrikin. They were the oddest pair and likewise perfect.

Kate thrived off adventure. Anna calculated the risk. I tagged along for the ride. Travelling on and off together for the better part of a month, the three of us hopped on buses, hiked in exotic places, camped in the wilderness and travelled to the southernmost part of South America, Ushuaia – the last stop before Antarctica! We'd pick berries and then I'd cook – preserves, jam roly-poly, rice pudding (our favourite). Haha – the kitchen wasn't their forte, but it was mine. We were quite the trio.

*Beauty and wonder filled our days,*
*but a relentless,*
*hidden emptiness,*
*filled my nights.*

At night, I'd recount the day. I'd silently analyse the women as they slept, I'd ponder how they could live so carefree. How they could be... happy. It baffled me.

The one thing I truly appreciated about these women was that they forced me to *live*. They lived. I went to places I never would have. I also learnt with great pleasure what a 'rucksack' was – a backpack. My word, the revelation had us all in fits of laughter.

Our last trek together was in Chile, Torres del Paine. What a riot of a time. With 160 km winds and jagged mountain ranges, we hiked for five days.

Before I left Australia, I was a little cheap. Not wanting to buy hiking boots that actually fit, I took Mum's. They were a size too big, but no big deal... an extra pair of socks would work?

Big mistake!

The combination of a 20kg backpack and rocky, mountainous terrain at death-defying heights – not to mention the wind and cold – meant my feet were having quite the workout.

**Day One**: Pretty good blisters were starting to develop.
**Day Two**: Blisters were well developed.
**Day Three**: My *entire* soles were HUGE blisters and I could no longer take my shoes and socks off. My skin peeled off with

the removal of my socks! Safe to say, I started sleeping with my shoes and socks on.

**Day Four**: I felt the most excruciating pain with each and every step. The terrain was *very* rough and jagged, meaning *more pain!* There was no way out of this hike other than getting to the other side. I had to do it.

It was time to suck it up, Princess!

The night of the fourth was one we would all remember...

We were attacked!

*We got into camp late, it was just nearing dusk. Night was settling in fast. Trying our best to find a flat space to set up camp, we got the tent up in record time.*

*Night had fallen and rain came.*

*Kate managed to boil water in the frigid weather. Anna had got things ready for dinner. I wearily wallowed as I nursed my sore feet.*

*Eating in our little two-man tent, it was cold!*

*We didn't bother with small talk, we opted for a very early night. We were exhausted.*

*Sleep came quickly for the sisters. One snored, the other happily joined and after what seemed like a lifetime of counting sheep, I drifted off as well.*

*Someone screamed!*

*Jostled and disoriented, our worst nightmare played out. It was 2am, and our tent was being attacked. Monstrous critters tried to eat and jump through the material of our tent.*

*It seemed we had unknowingly set up camp in the middle of a rats nest. They were huge! Huddled in the centre of the two-man tent, we switched on a tiny lamp. Anna squealed. Kate used her shoes to combat them. I sat and wallowed. My shoes were still stuck on my sore feet and I'd only just drifted to sleep.*

*My word, if someone had caught that scene on camera, we would all be famous.*

*Eventually the rats got the memo and left us alone. We threw our food out as a peace offering to them. They were appeased and the girls were pleased to sleep some more. Once again, I grumbled, "I'll never get back to sleep!"*

*A new day dawned before a new thought came.*

*Sleep came!*

**Day Five**: After a near sleepless night, day five turned out to be the toughest day by far, such a mental battle! There were flags to help guide the hikers and when seeing them all I could think was:

> *Bek, get to the next flag.*
> *No, the next one.*
> *Now, the next one...*

I had to keep my pace. Whenever I slowed down or changed pace the agony of those settling blisters was profound. The sisters, love them as I did, also liked to pace themselves, but we had **very** different paces.

My temperament was not very pleasant, especially when I'd wait for them. They told me to keep going, but I just couldn't seem to leave them behind.

Hour after hour passed.

EVENTUALLY WE MADE IT!

A wave of teary relief hit me when we saw the end.

*Civilisation!*

I think we were all **very** ready to part ways!

I walked through an incredible lesson – I could do so much more than I thought possible. I could endure **so** much more pain than I'd previously given myself credit for!

At the end of the day I'd made it – we all had!

Next time, however, I think I'll just hold off from scavenging my mother's hiking boots and buy my own!

Looking back at those memories, so much gratitude wells in my soul. I thank God for those women. They reminded me and they showed me how to **live**.

Anna, the doctor, recently passed away. As I remember her life and the memories we shared, I can't help but sadly smile. Kate and her sister shared a gift with me. When I felt I couldn't continue, unknowingly they showed me I could.

They unwrapped me a gift:

*Life.*

# A Riotous Time

God has such a sense of humour. We parted ways and riots broke out in the surrounding towns. Initially I was to take a bus north, but due to riots the bus turned into a boat!

The *Navimag.* It was a big, bad, rickety old cargo ship that cruised the glacial seas!

Like before, I made a few rookie mistakes... I forgot to check the weather forecast. Rocky seas is an understatement.

Grateful I could hobble through the ship by holding onto the walls of the narrow passageways, I enjoyed a hot meal in the dining room.

It was eerily quiet.
The dining room was nearly empty.
How bizarre.

*I heaved my way through that night.*
*Lesson learnt!*

The toilets were full from people being sick. I don't know how I made it through the night.

By coincidence – or 'God-incidence' – the boat was set to port in the Chilean village the Mennonites were ministering in.

Puerto Natales.
*(You've got to be kidding!)*

It had been over a month since I'd seen them and in reality, we'd only spent a few evenings together. Would they be waiting at the dock for me? It seemed so ridiculous, but I longed to see them. Why was I so terrified about being disappointed again?

Weary and with weak sea legs, I saw Jean and Kirsten waiting at the dock. I was amazed. I was scared. Hope involuntarily started to well within. I didn't know what to do with myself.

One thing I definitely felt amidst the fear was relief. At least I would have a place to lay my head for the night. Nervously, I followed them home. We arrived just in time for their prayer meeting. What was with me always turning up just in time for 'churchy stuff?'

The meeting was like nothing I'd ever encountered.

*I felt a thick presence of love.*
*It was both suffocating and beautiful,*
*I felt as though I was wading through a vat of fragrant oil.*

Overwhelmed and mortified, I found the longer I stayed in that environment the more emotional I became. Tears silently slipped down my cheeks. They seemed to flow faster and faster!

Eduardo the Chilean Pastor asked in Spanish to speak with me alone via Clayton the translator. I said I would, but knowing full well there was no way I'd let him. Why would I let this man talk to me alone, especially after a group of local South Americans tried to kill my sister and I in Peru? I don't think so! I had so little trust in men.

It was morning and upon leaving the Reach Team offered to take me on a mission call to an island. Nervous and excited, I went. We stayed late. Too late. I missed both buses. I stayed another night.

It was Sunday... just my luck,
**Church**!

Sitting next to me, Clayton quietly translated the sermon. The whole time I felt on the verge of tears. The weighty presence was back. I wanted to stay with the Mennonites. I didn't want to leave but likewise didn't want to be seen as taking advantage of them. Besides, I didn't know how to ask.

I felt such despair at the prospect of leaving.

In a desperate plea, internally I cried:

"God, if you're real, I want to stay with these people but I don't know how to ask. I can't see a way. Can you?"

The service ended and before I was swept up into the traditional post-church banter, Eduardo came to me and through Clayton said, "Rebekah, I must speak with you."

Jean was with us this time and nudged me:

"Rebekah, Eduardo was nice enough to open up his home to you. At least give him the respect of listening even if it means staying another night..."

It would.

When the crowd left, we spoke.

"Rebekah, the Lord told me to tell you this is your home if you want it to be – on one condition. You must live with the Mennonites, work with them and become part of their team."

I was gobsmacked. That was my exact prayer in Argentina. Eduardo managed to hear it from God, then Clayton translated it!

"God? You're real?"

# The Mission Within

My time with the Mennonites danced between feeling wonderful and sorrowful. A war raged within.

After spending a few weeks with the young 'Reach team,' I stayed with a Mennonite couple on a little island. Thereafter, I stayed with a different Mennonite family on another island.

We visited islands and villages. I learnt more of the language and met other Chilean families. Two months came and went in a blink.

It was an extraordinary season. I served with them, I served them and I encountered a tangible love I'd dreamt the Amish would have.

The first night with the Mennonite family was one I'll never forget. Dean, the husband, had the gift of 'sight' and saw my past. He shared the image he had, the name of the family member I needed to forgive and insight into my next season. Then he spoke healing and destiny over me.

"You will have a biological family."

I laughed and told him he had it wrong.

Doctors had previously told me I wouldn't have children. At nineteen and never having menstruated, I scoffed at the thought.

That night I was healed. My cycle began.

It was a night of many firsts. Dean's wife, Krystal, introduced me to singing in the Spirit. After receiving deliverance and once everyone had gone to bed, I heard and felt spirits around me. It was a night I'll never forget.

My eyes had opened.

Daily I sat, watched and listened. I spent time with Krystal and her brood and, honestly, it was beautiful. When our time together was nearing an end, a voice began to echoed within:

"Will you believe and follow Me, or not?"

I knew that God was real and had so much proof... but would I follow him? Could I? I'd been hurt by so many 'Christians.' Could I find trust there again?

The day before my departure all the Mennonites met at a stunning volcanic lake. It was overcast, it was cold and there I was baptised.

During my time with the Mennonites there was a constant litany of messages from home asking me to leave them, saying I was using these people like a leech sucks blood from a victim. Some said I was a coward and needed to learn to stand on my own two feet...

Grateful I stayed and with a renewed hope for my tomorrows, an impression was imprinted on my heart.

If I'm going to have children,
I want them to **go** for their dreams.
That means I can't be a hypocrite –
I need to go for mine too!
It also means I can't continue living this way...
this thorn in my side –
I **refuse** to pass it on!

With that, there was an all-encompassing reality, I needed to face my storm –

HEAD ON!

# Order in the Disorder

*Order in the Disorder –
it's time to step into the Eye of the Storm.
It's time to go into the Tornado of Chaos
and step into Clarity.*

*It's time to take courage and ride the storm,
because only then will you find the answer,
only then will you glean the key…
only then will you obtain victory.*

# Tornado of Chaos

I wish I could say that when I stepped back onto Australian soil everything was rosy and wonderful.

Newsflash! It wasn't.

It was hard. It was painful. It was horrid.

So much hadn't changed, while so much *in* me had. Being treated as though I was the same nineteen-year-old when I'd left, being chafed by the old and the new, I no longer knew where I fit.

Old patterns taunted, new desires hummed.

Turning down a degree in nutrition and dietetics, I held on to the last revelation in Chile – I had to GO for my dreams, not just follow an alternative route.

For six months, I worked hard! I sought out the best teachers, I saved every penny and invested it into music lessons, dance lessons and acting coaches.

It was time to pursue my craft.

Days were long. Nights were longer. I'd work by day in the nursing home, then travel an hour and a half into the city one way for lessons, or two and a half hours to the mountains by night. I sought wisdom from the best and life was constant!

Darkness would relentlessly try to discourage me. God seemed distant. Church was an unpalatable chore, but I felt I had to keep going.

Daily, I'd fight for freedom with food. I went to Reiki Masters. I went to acupuncturists. I sought hypnosis therapy and counselling. I went to prayer ministry and healing retreats. I had to be mentally prepared for the new journey – I had to break free.

It was obvious God wasn't breaking this stronghold – nor were any of the alternatives. Trying my best to hide the severity of what the disorder had become overseas, life was a relentless battle.

*Anticipation swept over me.*
*I picked up the letter.*
*With fumbling fingers,*
*I tore it open...*
*I got in!*

# Settling into the Storm

You would think living a life of alignment to the calling within would be easy, that it would be straightforward and rosy.

He says:

> *I am a light unto your path.*
> Psalms 119:105

Why doesn't a 'light' mean the illuminated path will be smooth?

Or the verse:

> *I will make your path straight.*
> Proverbs 3:6

It never mentions the path's incline rate?

Starting a musical theatre degree in another state and pursuing my dream should have been a season of wonder and bliss. Why wasn't that my reality?

I had found a church. I'd seen the favour of God getting me into the school – from finding out about the university a month and a half after late applications closed – and through the audition process. From reuniting with people I was well acquainted with in another life to finding the perfect home, then settling into that season – it was nothing short of miraculous.

Once I was settled, the real storm began.

It was to be three years of challenging debate, mental gymnastics, broken bones and uncovering a broken heart.

Knowing my beliefs, I'd also be posed with playing a certain character – naked.

"If you don't want to play it, you know where the door is!"

"Boys, I thought you were actors! Would you just look at her as though she's beautiful? **Act** as if she is! Okay, she might not be, but don't make it so obvious for the audience!"

Chin up, Bek.

Another lecturer's comment echoed within:

"No director will ever want to work with you. You're far too much work! If you can't trust a man, your partner, your fellow actor – there's no hope!"

Next role, a lesbian prostitute.

Played alongside my best friend, she whispered:

"You've struggled with men, but women haven't hurt you like that. You trust me. Let's show them what we can do!"

Top marks opened a Pandora's box.

The thing with performing and acting was I knew I could do it. I knew I was good, but it was the repercussions that held me back; the dreams, the nightmares, the memories.

I played the role. I shocked them all. But inside, a new battle began. Women were safe, men were not.

I tried to get support from church. It was as refreshing as drinking a glass of slimy water from a stagnant stream.

"This course is of the devil!"

"You need to quit, or you'll have a breakdown and it'll be your fault for not quitting now!"

Then from my pastor:

"You know Alex in youth? We all know he's gay. I just don't know how I should treat him... Should I just pretend he's not living such a life of sin? I don't understand how his mother can just leave him be. If he were my son, I certainly wouldn't!"

If she only knew my inner struggle... would she judge me too?

It was three of the most challenging years, but I won't pretend there weren't diamonds in the rough. I met some of the most inspiring directors and choreographers who pushed me beyond my limits and showed me new levels of capacity.

I met some lifelong friends like Sam, my house and classmate, not to mention the local beauties Rachel and Jess.

As precious as those blessings were they didn't negate the batterings or the storms I found myself in – they perhaps made them bearable.

Just.

# The Drag Queen and Conservative Christian

Who would have thought this unlikely pair of housemates would have such a riot of a time in their little cottage?

With many laughs we challenged all prejudices with our friendship. We were like the lion and the mouse. We'd share stories and cram during late night theory lessons (that I, of course, would teach). We played many practical jokes on each other and I would play as we would sing... what memories we made.

Beautiful but short-lived. Third year came and Sam moved on.

It was time for a change.

Dynamics shift at uni. Nothing remained the same.

In an environment so fixated on image, I could spot an eating disorder a mile away. By this stage mine had changed. I couldn't risk losing my voice again, so purging was replaced with hours at the gym. Daily 30km bike rides and 6km runs before uni. Then, there were night classes when I wasn't serving at church.

Comments by lecturers were constantly made over my fluctuating weight. My never-ending inner obsession reigned.

By the time third year arrived, I was amazed I'd survived that long!

The battle quickly intensified.

I watched my friends from afar. Once, we'd talk constantly. Now, that seemed a distant memory.

Silence.

Working alongside them was agony. I loved much, too much, and that was it.

They'd make the excuse that they couldn't stand *me* 'seeing' them, but I was sure it was *them* 'seeing' me that turned their heads and hearts.

One friend turned.

Another.

Sam didn't, but he was on his own journey. I let him go.

Church, likewise, pierced my heart.

"We only want you to play the piano.
How do you think we feel singing next to you?"

"You can sing, but just make sure you're quiet."

"Don't give her a mic!
If you do, make sure she's on mute!"

Would I ever fit in?

My Nan lived close by. She too never fit in – not in society or with family. Beautifully, we bonded. Living a life of distance meant we'd never spent much time together when I was growing up. Now in this season, we were finally able to close the gap. Mum and Dad started driving down every fortnight to look after her and years of brokenness and heartache slowly began to heal.

What a diamond in the rough.

# Fit like a Glove

Naomi attended Bible School in Byron Bay. After receiving such a breakthrough, she wanted me to meet the leaders who helped facilitate it. It just so happened that they were speaking at a conference in my neck of the woods...

There was no way in the world I wanted to go! I didn't particularly like church. I was tired and depressed. The **last** thing I wanted to do was be in a crowd full of eccentric strangers.

I said:

"God, I'm only going to this thing if it's $20 or less.
I'm poor and I'm not going to waste another penny on it."

It was $20.

It looked like I was going.

Dragging my feet, I arrived at a quaint little town in the middle of nowhere. I was amazed. It was close to where I'd been living and yet in all my three years of study, I'd never encountered it.

It was as though I'd stumbled upon an enchanted village.

Not knowing a soul, I arrived late to the conference.

There was one chair left – in the middle.

Grateful that everyone was already standing in worship, I was kindly ushered to a centre seat. Sadly, there would now not be access to a quick escape – great!

Begrudgingly, I started to sing. I looked around. There were some very interesting people there.

I won't lie, I was judging them all – left, right and centre. I wasn't the biggest fan of Christians at the time, and saw the lot of them as a tribe of hypocrites!

Fighting for composure, I drowned out the judgemental thoughts with the music... it was actually quite good.

A new thought entered:

"No one knows you here.
No one will stop you if you really *SING!*"

Closing my eyes, I allowed myself to be swept up in the sound. I let my voice soar.

*Involuntary tears started to fall.*
*I wept as I sang my gift back to God.*

The poisonous thoughts of other 'Christian' voices came to mind. Rising above, it was the first time I could look down on myself and see those poisonous darts for what they were. I saw the lies. I saw which ones hit the bullseye and which ones slightly missed.

Worship ended far too soon. Time stopped. I wanted to stay in that place of bliss forever.

When the evening ended, people came up to me. They'd thought the angelic hosts had descended when I sang.

They LOVED my singing, my gift...
They thanked me.

Well, that was a first!

Who would have thought my attendance at one little conference could change the next season of my life?

# Seasonal Shift

Week after week, I travelled to this town.

They had a midweek church-like service called *The House of Prayer*. I'd never been to anything like it. It was a whole night of worship where the songs would amalgamate from the prayers released. It was a completely new style of singing spiritual songs. Simultaneously artists painted, dancers danced and writers wrote.

*We collaboratively created an offering to God with the gifts he'd individually graced us with.*

*It was beautiful.*

Graduation was just around the corner and everyone was organising the next chapter in either Melbourne or Sydney. I felt God, who I called 'Pop,' say:

*You're moving here. You've had your worldly training in the arts, now it's time for your spiritual training.*

"Pop! What the heck?! NO, I'M NOT!"

The banter continued until I finally compromised:

"Fine! On one condition – two years **max**! I'm not doing another three year stint of study."

# The Two-Year Stint

L iving in the enchanted village was exactly that – enchanting. Surrounded by a forest, stunning lakes and healing springs, it was as though I was living in the midst of a fairytale.

Walking down the main road, I read something that emphasised that fantasy:

The Green Witch is in, come pick your potion.

In a community humming with occult, New Age and witchcraft, the veil in the atmosphere was thin.

I felt it.

On the other hand, it was extraordinary just how many period churches and parishes were there. They literally littered the streets. I often wondered if they were merely there to counter the seemingly counterfeit forces at play?

Honestly, I wouldn't be surprised. One thing I did find sad was that the majority of churches were either abandoned or renovated into homes. You could tell which force was seemingly 'winning.'

The spiritual community I found myself in, conversely, was very much alive. It was the first time I was unashamedly myself and accepted. It was wonderful!

Letting my voice soar above the congregation, my heart would sing! I would dance alone or with flags. I'd pull brothers and sisters out from the pews to join and we would literally shout for joy. I truly felt joy for the first time in a long while. It was glorious as we'd collaboratively create in that space.

It was as if heaven were colliding with earth.
Extraordinary.

There were times when I'd play the piano and my fingers danced with a skill that wasn't earthly. Or when oil would start pouring out of my hands and I'd see people healed. Or when I'd sing and hear the angelic hosts and join them. Or when I'd feel a presence next to me and my body would course with electricity and vibration.

It was such a special season.

Amidst the wonder there was also pain. At times, I'd be found weeping at the altar, trying to surrender a life of loss and shame. I didn't know how to allow myself to feel loved, or how to love.

Trust was huge in that season.

Just as musicians could synchronise with a glance, knowing where to go melodically or dancing together musically, this chapter became my season of syncing – with people, myself and God.

# The Synchronised Singer

Honestly, it's amazing to see how God transformed my life by harmonising a group of the most unlikely people with music. I learnt to read other musicians like never before. When we were in one accord in His presence, it was as though time stopped. We would be in an atmosphere of glory.

The quaint House of Prayer attracted musicians globally and before we knew it, the most beautiful German couple joined the team.

For a year, we worshipped together. I learnt so much from sitting under their anointing. The sets we played were positively beautiful. You could see and feel the atmosphere shift around us. I watched as they would manipulate the air with a single sound, be it produced by object or voice. They were so in-tune with the spirit, they could translate it musically.

I was in awe.

As a child, I'd always wanted to play the piano by ear. Mum, an incredible musician, can still play whatever tune you hum, in whatever key you wish. I'd always wanted to do that. My Nan, on the other hand, could play any note you placed in front of her – I'd always wanted to sight read like that too.

In this season, however, I learnt to play,
not by sight or sound:

I learnt to play by Spirit.

# Heart Strings

One afternoon, I sat at my keyboard. Overlooking the most glorious mountainous landscape, I cried out:

"God, teach me to play by ear. Teach me how to shift an atmosphere. Teach me how to escape into a melody."

I heard a faint whisper.

*What does the landscape make you feel?*

"I have NO idea!"

*Rebekah, stop. Look at it.*
*Close your eyes.*
*Now tell me,*
*what does it make you feel?*

"Peaceful?"

*What is the sound of peace?*

"How the heck should I know?"

*Find the note.*
*Close your eyes and find the frequency of peace...*

Slowly playing one note at a time, I went through every note on the piano. I found a few notes that seemed to fit... so I chose one.

Then He continued:

*What else do you feel?*

"Hope?"

*Find the note of hope.*

This continued until He asked me to weave the notes together. Slowly but surely, music emerged from within the setting.

It was an extraordinary exercise and although it took time I learnt how to hear, feel and translate. In The House of Prayer, He gave me a similar exercise – what do you *feel* in the spirit?

Now translate it into sound.

It was an incredible journey and not one I walked alone, for my housemate's sister had moved from America. With her arrival, I met a kindred spirit, a friend and a true blessing.

# Two Peas in a Pod

When I first met Cat I did not know what to think. She was a 'skinny minnie.' She had frizzy hair, a high-pitched laugh and a very squeaky voice.

Who would have thought we'd become two peas in a pod?

For a long season, I'd been put in the 'too hard basket.' It was cold, lonely and quite frankly miserable there. Little did I know, hidden within the woven strands of straw was a friend.

Cat and her sister had experienced a life of challenge and abuse. The thing that enraged me the most was that it was hidden behind a veneer of church leadership – their parents. They found it hard to trust, be seen and to be present. Yet still they had the most beautiful tender spirits.

Cat was an incredible musician. She played the drums, could sing a tune and tap the keys. What fun we had!

Wednesday night was our night to play in The Prayer House. The more we played and got to know each other, the easier it became to read each other's body language, strength of voice and touch of key. I'd look at her to start drumming, she'd close her eyes to start singing in the spirit. We would lead and follow each other instinctively. It truly was a beautiful musical dance we played.

That beauty didn't just stop in The House of Prayer. We started doing nearly everything together. She had a genetic condition, so not only was she constantly in pain, but at times had to strap her wrists and joints. Sometimes she'd struggle walking, other times she'd be so fatigued she could hardly get out of bed. The trauma and mental pain of her past didn't help with the physical pain of the now. I'd do my best to alleviate both by any means.

We'd walk side by side. I'd drive her to doctor appointments or to the grocers. We'd go on hidden adventures together and scour op shops. A lot of the time we didn't have to say anything to each other, but with a glance we knew how the other was feeling.

*It takes a lot of courage to be seen*
*after you've been in a life of hiding.*

Time with Cat and The House of Prayer became a beautiful restorative season. That became our song... until, of course, it was time to move on.

I'll never forget what it was like for that season to come to an end. I've never experienced such pain. Not only because I left in such a devastating way, but because this was a place where I finally felt at *Home*.

Two years came to a close and never would I have guessed that singing at a wedding would be the ultimate test.

Cat and I lived with Rose, the Pastor's daughter. She also played and sung in The House of Prayer, but never had she trained as a musician like us.

A wedding was the catalyst of a paradigm shift for us all.

It was the wedding of Rose's best friend,
Laura.

# The Aligning Stars

Laura lived in Brisbane. Her parents were down in Victoria and I was their gardener.

Her parents had the most exquisite gardens. From paddocks lined with lavender, to cast iron furniture hidden amidst the flower beds. It was like I was gardening in my own fantasy secret garden.

*Once more I was Mary in the Secret Garden,*
*I'd sing as I'd weed and water the earth.*

The beauty of the gardens was undeniable. Understandably, Laura wanted to be married in their midst. Her wish meant extra work for me, but I didn't mind. I'd dream about her day and pray over it while I worked.

With the day getting closer and all the preparations underway, Rose would practise her guitar every single day. She believed she'd be singing at Laura's wedding and wanted it to be perfect.

I understood and let the daily serenading outside my window slide. The challenge was, however, when the bride asked if I would sing at her wedding with one of her friends, James. Of course, I accepted thinking it was at the reception or an extra act to Rose.

Then she sent the songs. They were the same songs Rose had religiously been practising for months.

I was in trouble!

I'd just accepted her gig.

# The Other Wedding Singer

James met Laura in medical school. He was Nigerian and had a fancy for music. Laura and he were great friends during their university days in Wollongong and for years Laura had been *trying* to set both her best friends up.

Then I came along.

Not only had I taken Rose's gig, but it appears also the man she'd excitedly chatted to Cat and I about finally meeting.

"This could be the one..."

I couldn't have been in more of a pickle!

Introduced via email, James and I had a very rare and beautiful connection. The first email I received from him he signed off:

Jesus sets eternity in our hearts.

I was SO taken aback. That concept spoke to the essence of me and immediately I thought:

I'm not going to let him trump me.

So, I signed my first reply with:

God has made us gateways from Heaven to Earth.

Well, that was it. A new language was forged and from that point on emails were essays, phone calls were endless and days and nights were of one another.

Something special was brewing.

# The Cauldron of Calamity

As a child living in Nigeria, a member of James' family was murdered by a witch doctor. It's not my tale to tell, but the trauma left an imprint.

Now in Australia, I, his partner, was living where the atmospheric veil was thin. Very thin.

James was constantly on edge.

From unintentionally taking Rose's seat next to James' at the wedding reception, to the long distance relationship that blossomed thereafter, James constantly believed that Rose wanted revenge. He believed she was poisoned with bitterness and hate, that I was not safe.

Home dynamics changed. Dramatically!

Cat would dance between being an open book – something I'd pinned for – to being as closed as a coffin. Previously, I'd longed for Cat to open up and trust me with her story. Finally she was. I wanted to hold on to that, to nurture that. At times, she was closer than a sister and would cling to me physically and emotionally. At other times, she would hardly look at me and was as distant as a ship away from shore.

It was as though my heart was breaking.

James didn't like me talking to Cat. He didn't like our relationship and quite frankly that devastated me. How could he not see and understand the bond we shared?

Rose, on the other hand, enraged that I wouldn't share all that James and I discussed, turned into something otherworldly. I understood she was in pain, but the wounds she caused were deep. Very deep.

Daily James or his family would call and try to convince me to move. Rose would either kill, curse or poison me, or something of that effect would take place...

At the end of the day, I was not safe!

I was torn because I'd look at Cat, I'd feel her pain, but I no longer knew where my allegiances lay.

Our bond made James madder. He wanted me to have nothing to do with her – or them!

With so much turbulence, I sought God all the more. I started to have dreams. James had dreams. I was getting prophetic words left, right and centre, both from people I knew and people I didn't. I was searching the Word and crying out daily. Honestly, I thought James was who God had chosen for me, he was a rainbow to the stormy life I'd previously lived... that James was God outworking a promise to make beauty from ashes.

A ring appeared.

Home dynamics hit a new level of drama. At one point, my sister flew down from Queensland to help.

She arrived just in time.

# The Dress

My eldest sister was Maid of Honour. Mum thought it would help bridge our relational gap. It didn't. It was nearly more painful than the charade I was living through.

Sarah stood in unofficially. Flying down to help choose the gown, she was beautiful. The other girls, my Castlemaine friends, wanted nothing to do with it. That hurt but I was also so grateful I had kindred spirits elsewhere.

Sarah and I would walk and talk about life and my future. The joy that had been squashed by the girls would once again well up and overflow.

What a turbulent time!

Slipping into the elegant silk, feeling the stunning simplicity trail behind me – this was it.

I'd found my dress.

Arriving home, high and exhausted at the same time, I both wanted to share the news and didn't. When asked, however, if 'the dress' was found, I replied: "yes."

That night, blood was shed.

My heart bled.

I wanted there to be peace between us all again. Knowing my time with them was limited, I wanted to make the most of it, to cherish the memories and moments.

Willing to eat some humble pie, I went to talk with Rose. I was going to apologise for not being able to tell her everything, for causing her pain. I went to seek forgiveness and attempt to bridge the gap.

It didn't turn out well. Not well at all.

For two hours, I was locked in her room and her pent up anger reared its head. Her screams echoed throughout the house:

**"Your family threw you in the trash. We became your family and now you're throwing US in the trash. I can't believe you've turned into this deceitful woman, telling white lies and NEVER telling the truth! The WHOLE truth.**

**Who even ARE you?"**

Weeping, more was spoken, I could hear my sister pacing up and down the wooden hallway trying to get in. I could also hear Cat trying to calm and stop her.

By the end of it, I collapsed.

Bereft, hollow – I could no longer hold myself up. My sister just made it through the door. Picking me up, she too was crying.

"Bek, what can I do? Tell me, what can I do?"

I couldn't talk, walk or communicate.

Getting me into bed, Sarah held me. She cried.
I was speechless.

I'd shed all my tears.

I had broken.

Eventually, the situation was brought to light. My Pastors told me to forgive and forget. Rose had a right to speak her mind and if she'd caused pain, I should turn the other cheek. I understood she was their daughter, but still...

Turning not just another cheek but a new leaf:

I moved.

# The Family of Façades

With nowhere to go but north, I stopped for a short season back home.

Home was **very** different. The church asked if Mum and Dad would open their doors to an artisan Christian family of four. They were in need. My folks obliged.

Now entering a very shared space, things were vastly different. This family was beyond gifted. They were musicians, artists and creative performers. The wife, Jacqui, took to me and I to her. Sharing stories, fears and fates, she told me her story. She shared how God had told her to marry her husband. She told me of the brutal battles that resulted thereafter and she warned me of what was to come.

She was a lesbian.

She made moves. Children at one end of the house, we alone at the other end. In shock, I didn't stop her.

Running her fingers up my legs, my body responded. I'd never responded to James like this. Pure fear started to war within. Who was I?

I shared about my friendship with Cat. From that, Jacqui tried to convince me we were in fact in love. That I too was a lesbian and was about to 'ruin' my life, as she thought she had.

She whispered I would forever want to kill myself if I married James, so either I marry him quick smart, or not at all.

She was to be our wedding photographer.

With two little children in tow, I saw the torment in her eyes. Now I shared it. Not knowing who I was or what to do, I became terrified.

After bringing the story to light, I went on to face some substantial consequences.

I would be seen as a 'sexual predator' of my best friend. She wasn't allowed to see me alone, again. I would never hurt her, I loved her too much... but who would believe that now?

More confused than ever, I voiced my fears to James. I told him everything. EVERYTHING.

God had previously told me that my love for James would burn slow, that it would grow with time. But James was always jealous of my friendship with Cat. Now, understandably, that had heightened 100-fold!

He voiced how he felt. Of how I'd loved the moves Jacqui had made, supposedly welcomed them in fact. In honesty, I was shaken to the core. With a few caresses from this woman, my body responded like fire. On the other hand, with James it often felt like dread not desire. I'm an actress. He was always satisfied but I was forever hollow.

I didn't know what I was, who I was, or if what I felt was real or false. At the time, I had so much fear of men. Was that the reason my body didn't respond the same way to James? Was it merely previous wounds?

God help me!

I asked James for forgiveness, for him to be patient with me.

James forgave but never forgot.
I was not surprised, I understood completely.

My folks copped it too. They brought the situation into light at church, then a few months later a marriage ended.

What a mess!

What would they do with me now?

# The New Leaf

*A new life had begun.*
*It wasn't always easy*
*nor often fun...*

*In a land of dusty plains,*
*a land of muggy rains,*
*my little Toyota Yaris*
*entered the town of Tamworth.*

*When I first opened the door*
*of James' humble abode,*
*an odour knocked me over –*
*I thought I might implode.*

*It was a smell I had not known,*
*I did not know what to do.*
*Opening doors and opening curtains,*
*the pungent scent just wouldn't shoo!*

*So grateful that I was alone*
*and James did not see –*
*the shock, the horror I felt inside –*
*another tragedy!*

*Spraying scents, burning candles,*
*not much could be done...*
*It seemed this new chapter of my life*
*would have more challenging fun!*

*Straight to work, spray in hand,*
*I scrubbed the whole house down...*
*Washing clothes, washing sheets*
*until squeaks were the resounding sound!*

*As time past by*
*my nose did adjust,*
*I'd venture out alone –*
*with more of James' trust.*

*It was time to make this house of mine*
*a beautiful, comfortable home.*
*It was time to let go of what was behind*
*and not feel so alone.*

*We bought a table, we bought some chairs,*
*so we'd eat not on the floor.*
*And when James would leave for work,*
*I too would leave to go explore.*

*I went to make friends,*
*I went to find work,*
*I went to not feel so alone...*
*As days and weeks passed on by*
*I still missed those from my previous home.*

*James was not happy,*
*he was not impressed...*

*Why couldn't I leave them behind?*
*But how could I get him*
*to understand how I pinned?*

*I pinned for my friends,*
*I pinned for the life*
*that saw me singing and dancing*
*with pure delight...*

*I wanted him to understand,*
*to cherish the life I loved –*
*I wanted him hold me tight.*

*I tried so very hard*
*to let that life go,*
*to not look back into my past*
*so those longings would not grow.*

*I tried to look ahead and dream*
*of all that was to come,*
*to leave the past far behind,*
*pressing onward into the sun...*

*But the weather here was new for me.*
*The air was hot, sticky and thick!*
*I missed the cool bite of the wind,*
*was this all another trick?*

*Another challenge I had to face*
*seemingly alone.*
*For James would work day and night,*
*very rarely was he home.*

*I was terribly fortunate though
for some lovely people I met.
They listened to the stories of my past
so I wouldn't forget...*

*They helped me be grateful
for all that was and all that would be...
They encouraged me to dream again
and to try and be happy.*

Life in this new land was foreign, lonely and disconcerting. Dramatic as it may sound, I knew if I didn't quickly adapt, I wouldn't make it.

Working to establish a community, to get to know the neighbours, I joined a gym, I looked for work, I planned a wedding and I went to church.

I had to believe there was blessing in the midst,
that hope was merely hiding.

As an emergency doctor, James was constantly working **long** hours. Our relationship became strained from the previous months and internally I fought resentment that he never really took the time to invest and get to know *my* people. I always knew I was going to move closer to him but had we been open and honest about everything, my friends and my spiritual family wouldn't have been so hurt. I wouldn't have been so shunned.

Deep down, I believed he was a major catalyst of the ruin.

Even though vows weren't spoken, I started to dutifully fulfil my 'wifely' duties – cooking, cleaning and making a home. Before I arrived, for over a year James slept on a blow-up mattress and ate on the floor. There was quite a bit of homemaking to do!

People told me we would never work. Rose mentioned it once or twice herself. Stubborn, fiery and determined, I wanted to prove them all wrong!

I'd chosen my bed.

Now I would sleep in it.

# The Battle

*The battle in my heart real,*
*the pain in my spirit raw.*

*Try as hard as I may*
*the residue I could not ignore.*

*Daily I would weep,*
*daily I would bleed.*

*Was I truly following God?*
*His steps did I honestly heed?*

*I'd pray both day and night,*
*I'd try to submit my will.*

*Did I get it wrong?*
*Would He graciously fulfil*

*The desires of my heart*
*that were bleeding, broken and lost?*

*Looking, I couldn't fathom*
*the sacrifice and cost!*

*Now all on my own,*
*no friend to call and chat.*

*I wished and yearned I hadn't left,*

*I wanted to go back...*

# Two to Tango

I may have decided to sleep in the bed, but it takes two to tango!

*The wedding just around the corner,*
*a few sleeps to go.*
*We would fight on and off –*
*did he love me?*
*I didn't know.*

*I stopped doing the little*
*obligatory chores instead,*
*I tried to remember who I **was**,*
*I had to get out of bed!*

*I couldn't be the Nigerian wife*
*he expected me to be.*
*It had become a noose,*
*I needed to be me!*

*He didn't like this woman,*
*the one before his eyes.*
*I wish the news wasn't*
*such a distasteful surprise.*

*He had his mother call*
*my dad to formally say,*
*he would not be attending*
*our planned wedding day...*

*I didn't love him enough,*
*I caused him too much strife.*
*He was worried he'd be cursed*
*if I became his wife!*

*Dad didn't tell me,*
*it was for James to do.*
*Why am I still surprised*
*he never followed through?*

*The dad and daughter fought.*
*"No, the wedding is going ahead!*
*We're taking this weekend to pray."*
*That was all we said.*

*We needed a little space*
*before the wedding day.*
*"Dad – you've got it wrong!"*
*"Rebekah, it's the **other** way."*

*Blood boiled in my veins,*
*a tear tore through my heart.*
*So much for the two of us*
*being destined, set apart...*

*He couldn't find it in him,*
*to share that truth with me...*
*All I'd sacrificed and lost,*
*what stupidity!*

*The pain of that rejection*
*was severe, it cut me deep.*
*I would thereafter be tormented*
*both conscious and asleep.*

*With nowhere to escape*
*with nowhere left to go,*
*the pain and the despair*
*began to manifest and show.*

*My flesh would be aflame,*
*it would burn like fire.*
*An emptiness gnawed within,*
*it would grow each passing hour.*

*I was hollow, full of dread –*
*alive but likewise dead!*

*Panic seeped its way*
*into my reality.*
*Fear gripped me like a vice*
*chained in captivity.*

*There was nowhere left to go,*
*what a failure I'd become.*
*It seemed no one understood,*
*I'd watch the setting sun.*

*It did nothing.*

*Beauty – I knew it was*
*but it was too far away.*
*I couldn't touch it,*
*I couldn't embrace it.*

*This world I didn't belong.*

*If I didn't do something quick*
*very soon I would end...*
*God, where were you in my midst?*
*That constant faithful friend.*

Weeping, I would sing. I would scream and proclaim the goodness of God even though my life only reflected disaster. I would prophesy hope when all I felt was despair, still I'd hold on. I had to hold on, it was all I had left:

*Faith.*

# The Dark Horse Comes

*He tells me all that I am,*
*I feel it in my bones, in my blood.*
*I look in the mirror and choose.*
*I **am** His daughter,*
*I **am** part of His royal priesthood.*
*I **am** beautifully and wonderfully made,*
*I AM His.*

Words, words, words. What good are they? My life was in absolute disarray! I needed help, hope and I needed light.

It was the eve before the supposed wedding. In the midnight hours I snuck out of the Airbnb to visit my previous Pastors. I knew I was going against my family's wishes but I just needed some peace. How I'd missed them.

"Rebekah, if you'd just listened to us, you'd never be in this mess.
You're not going to get whole unless you move back here and
we put you back together again.
We love you, but this is your doing.
You were warned!"

So much for getting peace. It was the last time I'd visit.

Though the wedding was over, a non-refundable policy meant the 'reception dinner' would go ahead. With strong family values, Dad said I was to attend. I had an obligation to honour the guests who had flown over.

A rage warred within. A brokenness. Unwilling to show the utter wretchedness I felt in my heart, I painted my lips in blood red and entered in a black dress.

As soon as everyone departed, I felt more emptiness in my heart than I ever thought possible. I was so utterly hollow. Regardless, life went on and I had to face reality. It was time to fly back 'home.' But, where was home?

Driving from Brisbane to Tamworth, I nabbed a speeding fine before entering an empty house.

It was time to move out!

Where would *my* home be now?

I couldn't return to my parents' house, not after everything with Jacqui's family. The loneliness and pain I experienced there was palpable. Now my desperation was palpable.

Staying in a granny flat in Tamworth, I had a few weeks grace. I had to figure out my next move, I also had to do it in haste!

I seemed to be frozen in an icy darkness and pain. I didn't know how to escape. Bulimia came back with a vengeance. Previously, I used exercise and other methods to combat a binge. It was no longer enough.

I needed the vicious barbarity bulimia brought.

Wrapped in more shame, I became a living corpse. I would hide by day, sneak out at night. If I saw anyone I knew, they got quite a fright for I was unsightly!

Fear wrapped around my throat. I didn't know if I could go on.

Emptiness called.
Silence taunted.
Sleep.
I needed sleep.

# Lasso Life

The clutches of shame are powerful. The claws of deceit, talons of guilt and clench of despair suffocate – their ultimate mission is to destroy.

I was in the ditch of despair, wading in the wallow. It was cold, muggy and dark, the weight in the air was thick and heavy.

I was exhausted and battle weary, my being wanted to surrender and to be swallowed by the waters of wallow.

I couldn't see a way forward. Hope was slipping out of my grasp, courage too. Fear bombarded like a plague...

> "You will never overcome."
> "You will never escape."
> "No one cares."
> "You're alone!"

I couldn't see the light. I couldn't see a path ahead. I didn't want to continue, but I knew if I stopped I would never go on.

I was on a path with no return. Not many had weathered the journey to reach its end. Many had succumbed to the waters of despair. Many were tortured beyond recognition by constant taunting. Many gave up and gave in, just before the border of breakthrough.

Pressure built up in my mind and body. Weary, I stumbled and fell.

Smeared with dirt, blood and tears, I wanted to give in... but then I felt the caress of my calling.

The quiet whisper of my destiny echoed through my mind...

"Keep going."
"You're nearly there, don't give up!"
"The border is just ahead!"
"You were born to overcome and win."
"You are not alone!"

Unsure if it was a memory, a reality or a dream, these thoughts invaded my mind like a subtle vapour.

I pressed on.

Each step took more effort than I knew I possessed. My will was reignited – there was no other choice but to make it. My destiny lay in the balance. This is what I was born to champion, fight and win.

I was nearly there...

I had to believe I was nearly there.

I chose to believe I was nearly there...

Just one more step.

Just one more choice.

Reach just a little bit further.

Turning off all other sounds – the pain, the insufferable emptiness, the gnawing of defeat, the constant taunting, the lies, the heat, the stench of darkness – I chose to do one thing. Believe.

I knew I was born for this. I knew I was not alone.

I knew we would win.

We had to.

There was no other choice.

My mind started to fog. It started to spin.

Trying to steady myself, there was nothing to grasp.

I reached...

I stumbled...

I fell.

Exhausted, I tried to get up but the sludge swallowed my legs and body.

Fear stole my breath.

I was sucked into a quicksand of shame.

Would this be my end?

Closing my eyes, despair nearly stole my destiny.

Then I remembered...

Destiny.

This was **not** my destiny.

NO! This wouldn't be my end.

With a strength that I knew not I possessed, something from within my spirit raged.

Power from beyond the veil of consciousness propelled me forward.

The sludge no longer stuck, the pit was no longer bottomless.

It became easier.

I was wading into shallower waters.

The swamp was thinning...

Light.

I could see a speck of light.

Just a glimpse, but it was on the horizon.

The border was right ahead.

I would make it.

I had to make it.

Blinding my sight to see only the light, I ploughed through the fields of defeat.

With a cry of joy, my feet gathered speed. Hope welled from within my soul.

I was nearly there.

Deceit tried to claw at me. The shackles of shame attempted to rope around my ankles, but they failed.

Darkness failed.

The heat and light were too bright!

Waves of peace washed over me. Encouraged me.

Cleansed in the tenderness of light, in the gentleness of love, I had made it.

*I had to fight to live,*
*fight to breathe,*
*fight for breath!*

Worried after not hearing from me, Sarah my sister called.

"Bek, I've been doing some research. Why don't you do a Jillaroo School or something? You've always wanted to work with horses... go and see what's out there. I'm sure there's something close by, you're in horse country after all. I'm happy to pay for it."

I didn't want a bar of it – of anything – but eventually I complied.

I found a school.
Leconfield.

A new class was about to begin. I'd be leaving within the week.

# Classroom of Cows

Still hollow and just weeks after the move, my life was again about to shift. But I didn't want to bring any emotional baggage, I didn't want people to *see* me. I didn't like that I was alone without a place to go. Regardless of how I felt, I went.

Every day on the station, I would hike up a mountain and pray:

"Lord, please let me see the beauty in the insignificant.
Let me make that insignificant, significant.
Show me light."

There was literally so much darkness within me I had to fight to find and see light.

One morning after my hike, I saw a woman trying to do some stretches. I tell you, she was doing them **all** wrong – I had to show her the right way.

My jeans split! For **all** to see.

In that split second, I could choose mortification and humiliation or humour. I chose the latter. Joy.

Boy, did we laugh!

Quick smart, I had to find a pair of jeans in the rag bin for we were about to muster the cattle on horseback. Scouring through the rag bin, a meagre shift began.

*The old has gone,*
*disappeared, destroyed –*
*as far as the East is from the West,*
*I am told.*

*Erased from the book,*
*erased from His mind.*
*When He looks at me,*
*what does He find?*

*A completed work,*
*destiny unveiled.*
*Light, love –*
*darkness failed.*

*Power untold, power undone;*
*power a gift from the Son.*

*Courage to walk,*
*courage to see*
*all I was created to be.*

*A knowing that He is by my side,*
*a knowing that forever He will reside.*

*A knowing that all I have to do*
*is stay, dwell, be made new.*

*Day by day, renew my mind*
*until the lies I no longer find.*

*Transformed by His glory and grace*
*with wisdom to change the human race.*

*Choosing to turn away from the past,*
*abiding in His love that lasts.*

*Choosing to stand firm saying "No,"*
*darkness will and must then go!*

*The power is there,*
*the strength will come –*
*I just need to spend time*
*with the Son.*

*He has given all I need,*
*His words I just need to heed.*

*Leaving the ways of the world behind*
*so the remnants of death I no longer find.*

*Turning from all that was before,*
*pressing onto a brand new door.*

*Walking the path that's narrow and hard,*
*choosing to abide with the one who's scarred.*

*Keeping my eyes solely on Him,*
*leaving what had always been.*

*Choosing to believe I AM a Queen*
*even if I have not seen*

*the fruit, the power,*
*His Almighty hand.*
*I choose to become all He planned.*

*I choose not to follow the ways of before*
*but to continue into the new and explore.*

*I choose to follow what's timeless and lasts,*
*I choose to leave the past in the past!*

*I choose to be strong regardless of fear,*
*His voice alone I choose to hear!*

*I choose not to side with despair,*
*I choose to be free without a care!*

*Embracing the day, expectation in my heart –*
*this joy I feel I want not to depart.*

*I choose to be all He created me to be –*
*glorious, beautiful, completely set free!*

I started to get back on the horse. I started to ride through life, little by little, day by day...

Why was it that as soon as I'd found my footing, something else would happen? Something would cause me to slip, considerably!

I met a boy:

William.

# Will a Way

*If there is a Will
there is a way,
unless the Will wants not to stay.*

Meeting at the station, he looked the part. Akubra, jeans, RM Williams belt, cheeky grin and killer dart striker. Will waltzed into my life.

He was a great guy and funny friend, but when I looked closely I saw pain in his eyes. I knew he was running. I knew he was hurting. I knew he'd drown it with a drink or two.

We'd talk by the campfire, play darts with Ally and Broughton. He would beat us hands down, blind drunk or not – it was station living.

Riding a horse. I can honestly say that's where his façade fell to the floor – he was woeful! With reins rattling in the wind, his arms flapping and tongue clucking, anyone who watched could not help but smile. He'd have a ball, but there was no way he'd be able to muster a steer, bull or even a small heifer.

Ally was naturally inclined to Broughton and Will seemed to fancy me. Honestly, I couldn't handle anything more than a friendship. More is what he wanted.

"I just want to make you laugh, make you smile.
Do you know how happy it makes me when you do?
Let me.
Give me a chance."

Struggling to keep myself afloat, there was no way I'd be able to carry another. I was merely weeks out of not being wed. I was **not** interested.

We parted ways soon after I drew a clear line in the sand.
School had ended.

He parted life a few days later.

His family...

It seems he'd told his family all about the singing jillaroo he'd met.

I was to meet his family very soon thereafter.

I wrote a piece to be performed at his funeral.

I was a mess.

It didn't help when a grieving family member said:

"If you'd just said yes, Will would still be here."

I had to fight for life. Unfortunately, William couldn't fight any longer. I couldn't take that guilt on board. I already carried a weight too great to bear alone. Once again, with nowhere to call home, I wept. I didn't know what to do or where to go. I was floundering in an empty abyss.

Where was GOD?

# The Dreamer and
# the Dream

*The gift of a gesture,*
*the power of a word.*
*In action, you hear*
*a statement, it's heard.*

*Calling to not merely*
*the mind and the heart,*
*but calling much deeper*
*where the dream did start.*

*To the Dream.*

*When you see others*
*dream, lift and fly*
*it's not easy to watch*
*them pass you by.*

*The happiness and joy*
*enough to tickle and annoy*
*is brewing in the wake –*
*make no mistake.*

*But within the sight,*
*within the dream*
*a tug pulls on your heart.*

*Are you ready to let them go?*
*For them to finally depart?*

*Another tug pulls.*
*Were you even there?*
*The influence of your life,*
*will you be able to share?*

*In this new chapter,*
*in this new day,*
*or in love must you let go?*
*Let them blossom into what they're to become –*
*let them live, dream and grow.*

*Knowing they will be away from you,*
*not being by their side,*
*a tingling flutters within your heart –*
*a need to say goodbye.*

*A need to champion them on their way*
*into the unknown,*
*a need to release them into His hands –*
*let them finally find their home.*

*Not just in the physical sense*
*but in the deeper call of their heart,*
*for when they follow the dream within*
*the path to home does start.*

*They didn't realise they were lost*
*or that they were alone.*
*But finally in the heeding of their dream*
*they found their way back home.*

# Glowing Feet

I was surrounded in an abyss of darkness. It was cold and the air was thick. I could taste fear. I didn't know where to go. I wanted to run and hide, but there was no escape. I was in the valley of the shadow of death.

He spoke of this valley and of this darkness. He also mentioned that it was a shadow of death – not death itself.

*Even though I walk through the valley of the*
*shadow of death, I will fear no evil, for you are with me,*
*your rod and your staff they comfort me.*
Psalms 23:4

He said I would walk through it. He also said I wouldn't feel evil. He implied that it was my companion that calmed my fears. Was it because he had a rod to ward off attacks and a staff which would lead me into provision?

I tell you, regardless of what the Word said I **felt fear** as real as I feel these keys under my fingertips. It was real. It was palpable. And I couldn't seem to see, feel or sense Him!

How could I not feel the evil? Will was dead, James long gone, Cat wouldn't speak to me. I couldn't go home. How was I supposed to feel Him in the midst of all this pain?

So much for an Almighty God!

Was it merely a choice to believe my companion would be both my sight and security?

I didn't like that thought. The thought that although I was no longer alone, I was still travelling blind... I wouldn't be riding with the reins but would have to trust my steed completely.

A scripture came to mind:

> *I will be a lamp unto your feet.*
> Psalms 119:105

Great. So I'd have glowing feet but there would still be an abyss of darkness.

Fine!
I'll stop grumbling and I'll put on those ruddy shoes of peace!

As soon as I'd made that decision a stillness swept over me. I was grounded in peace. It was quite extraordinary. I didn't know where I would go. I didn't know what I would do. And although fatigue hung around like morning sickness, there was hope.

Why hadn't I done this earlier?
Sheer stubbornness!

I realised then that 'walking by faith and not by sight' was indeed possible when my feet were glowing with the peace of the King of Kings.

Then, as I glanced down towards my glowing feet, I saw another pair of toes shadowing mine.

I may not have been able to see the person. I may not have been able to see my surroundings but in that instant I knew all would be okay. I knew I would make it through. I knew I was not alone.

*I will never leave you nor forsake you.*
Hebrews 13:5

I *knew* I was not forsaken. I felt it in the deepest part of my being. My circumstances could have suggested differently but I was not my circumstances. I was a daughter. God's daughter.

With a shaky breath, I held my head up to the darkened sky. I boomed with a voice, not shaky but strong:

"I will NOT be afraid. I will NOT give in! An army of heavenly hosts surrounds me. They will conquer you demonic ghosts! My God is right here. He is by my side, and we will transform to day this nigh!"

*Thank you, Pop. Thank you, Father. That although I can be stubborn, although I can see the waves and the storm around me, you teach me to walk on water – to know the truth.*

*Help me, Lord.*

# Floundering Fatigue

*There is an*
*incredible fatigue.*
*Tossed by a mighty wave in a raging sea,*
*I'm engulfed.*

*Floundering, spluttering,*
*desperate for a break in the break of the waves,*
*none comes.*

*Wave after wave,*
*muscles pricked by millions of pins.*
*Muscles heavy as lead,*
*weary, exhausted,*
*I dread rising from bed.*

*Little sleep has come,*
*another day's begun,*
*a need to carry on,*
*to fight and to stand up strong...*

*But now no light is left.*
*I've fought a war,*
*I've done my best.*
*I know not what to do.*
*I sink into the abyss*
*that's fierce, vast, that's blue.*

*In that moment of surrender,*
*in that moment of release,*

*the raging waves calmed,*
*the howling winds ceased.*

*Peace.*
*Stillness.*

*Calm came with a drizzle of rain.*
*It was not death I welcomed*
*but hope:*
*Life.*

*A boat drifted by.*
*Saved, I let out a sigh.*
*A hand reached out for mine,*
*and what I did find*
*was the eyes of a Father.*
*A heart that was aflame –*
*passion, love and laughter,*
*He called me by my name.*

*As he pulled me into*
*the little wooden boat,*
*I was pleasantly surprised –*
*it was sturdy and afloat.*
*Cocooned by a blanket,*
*a hot drink to warm my hands,*
*with pride, He started to share*
*all that He had planned.*
*He was joyous I would let him*
*row me safely to the shore.*
*Warmed and safe I closed my eyes,*
*it was time for rest and not much more.*

# The Subtlety of the Snake

It was hard to trust God when I was constantly in a graveyard. Be it of dreams or life, loss felt to be a constant theme in my life.

My friends from the past seemed to be as transitional as seasons. They would only stay until suited. I would love and love fiercely, only to be left thereafter. Still, I gave the benefit of the doubt. I'd call and try to reach out...

Perhaps selfishly.

I needed and yearned for their love. For love.

I hadn't heard from them in weeks – nearly months. The longer the calls went unanswered, the more the messages awaited response, the heavier the feeling of abandonment.

I was too much...
I wasn't worthy...
I was a constant headache to all I loved...
It was my fault...
I was too needy...
Our friendship, like all friendships, had a 'use-by date.'
This one had merely reached its expiration.

I was hurt but I was like a dog to a bone – I wouldn't give up! I wouldn't accept the reality that they were gone. I kept calling. Every time a message or call was left without a response, a deeper tear tore.

One more time.

I decided to call one more time and then I'd put it all to bed.

It rang.

Again and again.

*Ring ring... ring ring...*

Silence.

With a deep breath, I lay my phone aside and said:

"That's enough now."

Instantly they responded!

I was shocked and overjoyed.

The months of silence were a distant memory – forgotten in an instant!

Picking up where we left off, it was wonderful. The lies that seemed to chorus through my mind were revealed for what they were – lies. I'd been listening to the songs of deceit on repeat and disappointment dissolved instantly. My friend had been on her own journey.

I was shocked at how subtly the snake could use a season of silence.

I had been taunted – constantly.
Relentlessly.
Lonely.
Hurt.
Past wounds would play jovially on repeat.
I was being suffocated.
My worth, self-esteem and confidence lay in the answering of a call.

What power I gave my mobile!

I realised I had placed that same power in my friends' hands.

*Their reception was the measurement of my worth.*

How ridiculous, yet how revelatory.

The enemy had slyly slithered between my wounds, reminding me how let down I had been, how unworthy I was and why my circle had constantly been broken.

Truth be told, my worth, confidence and life needed to come from the Lord – not man.

I would beat myself up for falling short. I would become disgusted at who I was. Playing that ugliness on repeat, I'd sabotage every success.

Then I remembered:

*The enemy comes to steal, kill and destroy...*
John 10:10

It didn't matter if I self-destructed, it made an easier job for the enemy!

*He is the Father of all lies.*
John 8:44

I listened to his voice, rather than that of my Father.

I had to recalibrate.
I had to refresh, restart and renew my mind.

Waking up, I realised I needed to start the day how I wanted my victorious self to start it. I needed to act how my victorious self would act.

I had gained weight. I was exhausted, physically and emotionally. I was unhappy with my appearance. But, I got up.

My victorious self would love herself, be proud of herself, look after her temple – so that was what I would do. That was how I would see myself!

I didn't have to exercise at full capacity. I didn't have to wear the size I would eventually wear once more. I just had to start.

**So**, I got up. I gave what little of the morning I had left to Pop and decided that today I was going to walk as He says I can walk.

Today, I'm going to walk free!

# Changing Tides

*Change never comes easy.*
*It's painful,*
*it takes perseverance*
*and more often than not, it's ugly!*

How could I change a lifetime of pain?
How could I shift from a victim mentality to a victor reality?

I had **no** idea.

In need of a little encouragement, just a drop of hope, I scrolled through videos on YouTube. I came across a testimony. It was from a woman who had survived and suffered so much more that I could ever comprehend.

She was Jewish.

I listened to her tale of horror. It seemed impossible to fathom. From death camps, torture and starvation, to the torment of entertaining the torturers. I looked at this survivor and her mother's last words echoed through my mind:

"No one can take away from you what you've <u>chosen</u> to put into your own mind."

The word *chosen* rang as clear as a day.

I'd always known the battle was within, a year in an asylum was enough proof. I've read the words, time and time again,

*Only think on what is good, pure and holy.*
Philippians 4:8

*Meditate on the Word day and night.*
Joshua 1:8

But honestly, what good was that? Seventeen years later I was still fighting those same demons. I would proclaim and claim those so-called 'promises,' but what good did it ever do?

Why did I never change?

Sitting in front of me was a little old lady on a screen. In this fierce little survivor, I saw the fruit of that scripture. The torture, the torment, the slave training didn't transfigure her spirit, for she held onto the words of her deceased mother – she **chose** to remember **who** she was.

Who was I?

Of course, distress would come with despair and a longing to surrender, but those thoughts she would catch and change. She had to snatch them before they would transform her mind and heart forever.

*Life and death is in the power of the tongue.*
Proverbs 18:21

Likewise, the thoughts you grasp onto...

**Make** *your thoughts captive.*
2 Corinthians 10:5

She had to curtail the influence of her environment so as not to destroy her inner world.

I had to do the same.

*For years I had read the Bible, but was I truly led by it?*

# Cultivating the Culture Within

Was a lack of freedom the fruit of my lack of perseverance in the Truths of God?

*Do not merely listen to the word, and so deceive yourselves.*
***Do what it says.*** *Anyone who listens to the word but does not do what it says is like someone who looks at his face in a mirror and after looking at himself goes away and immediately forgets what he looks like. But whoever looks intently into the perfect law that gives freedom and continues in it – not forgetting what they have heard but doing it – they will be blessed in what they do.*
James 1:22–26.

Little by little, I became more and more convicted. Yes, change needed to happen but it wasn't the external home that was in dire straits, it was my internal home.

My temple, His temple.

*It's easier to know who you're not than who you are.*
*Stop listening to the accuser, stop listening to the lies!*

For years, a voice would not cease. It would call to my failings and it would lie. The problem was that I listened.

I meditated in a mindset of decay. I needed to stop.

I needed to cease listening to the lies and say goodbye to the excuses and reasons I'd find myself stuck in a hole. It was time to climb out of the tomb. It was time to become whole!

The question was, how?

How would I effectively change decades worth of negative patterns? How could I attune my ear to only hearing the truth?

I had lived a life of defeat. I didn't know how to stand as a victor rather than a victim. But too much had been stolen, too little was left.

Remembering the testimony of the Jewish survivor, I held onto her story and her victory. She became a token of hope. Yes, she still had to battle. Yes, she had been tortured daily. But, it was what she did with her daily thoughts that mattered.

In the midst of not knowing where to go or what to do, I heard God tell me:

*Rebekah, you need to write from victory, into victory. You need to write through your failings and show my grace and then you need to extend that grace to yourself, until you become the living testimony of it.*

# A Living Testimony

Eventually, I found my way home. *Home, home.* Riddled with memories, woven with grief, it was honestly the last place I wanted to be, but what choice did I have?

I'd tried living out of my car but after getting my tyres slashed while sleeping, I realised it wasn't the best option long term.

An opportunity arose in Sydney to audition for *Jekyll & Hyde: The Musical*. What did I have to lose? Honestly, nothing! My pride was already pretty abysmal if it didn't work out.

Mum and Dad graciously opened their doors, so it was decided. After an eighteen-hour journey, I walked through the audition room doors.

The audition was not what I expected, especially when I was posed with the question of why I thought I could play Emma, Dr Jekyll's fiancé...

"Well, I was just engaged to a doctor, so I know what that's like. After we got engaged, he kind of changed from Jekyll to Hyde, so I know what that's like. My fiancé left just before the wedding, and in the musical Dr Jekyll dies on their wedding day. I can tell you I'm so fine with that too. At least I'll be able to wear a wedding dress this time round!"

Not knowing how to respond, jaws dropped and giggles erupted.

The door opened. I got the role.

For the next four months, I would be singing my story on stage.

Jake played Dr Jekyll and when we'd sing together, it was honestly like milk and honey. I shared some of my story with him.

"Rebekah, I would have fought for you.
I would never have done that."

His partner sat in the audience. My heart started beating for him. Wrong, but extraordinary. My thoughts became strings of poetry. Never was I a poet before I met Jake.

When day turned to night and the woman beside him slept, messages would start. Wrong again, but the story we performed was so close to my previous reality. He – a kinder face. His voice – richer. His power – stronger.

I then got myself very much in a pickled sandwich. I'd composed music for him and after receiving his response, giddy as a schoolgirl, I took a screenshot and sent it to a girlfriend in the show.

To my horror, I'd mistakenly sent it to the ENTIRE CAST!

Talk about being sprung!

To say I was mortified is a gross understatement and in the days when you couldn't delete a Facebook message, there was nothing I could do but bear the brunt of the consequence.

His partner came to every show thereafter and even though there was a whiff that he'd leave her, I soon realised it was mere fantasy.

So, I did.

In my little two-door Toyota Yaris, I drove back to the countryside.

It was time to be a jillaroo again!

Nothing about that season was victorious, other than perhaps losing a lot of weight and not in a particularly healthy way.

A victorious life was still very much a foreign concept. The panic attacks I suffered on arrival home eventually subsided, the humiliation of walking into the family church without a ring and a man dwindled, and soon the whole Jacqui charade started to calm as well. But still, the storm within my soul never seemed to dissipate.

I honestly didn't know if it ever would.

# Barren Pains

Driving around the countryside just me, myself and I, anything was possible. I could go anywhere I wanted. I could be whoever I wanted. No one would be the wiser.

It didn't matter how far I drove, I found I couldn't drive out of my pain. My loneliness. My shame.

So much for living victoriously.

I would write about the journey. I would paint a picture of the wonder and awe of the countryside but within my heart, within my hands, there was nothing.

I'd made it to the cattle station in the north of the Northern Territory. The nearest town 100kms away consisted solely of a pub!

I was in the middle of no man's land.

Being both the station hand and cook, my hours were longer than everyone else's and my workload too. Okay, so perhaps I didn't do all the heavy lifting the men did but I'd have to rise before them, cook for them, prepare lunches, go out with them, come back, cook dinner, keep a clean kitchen and cool room, butcher the beasts, do a stocktake, not to mention make fortnightly orders!

It was a lot, but it was cathartic – working hard.

I learnt so much about doing bore runs, oiling utes, driving the semi, re-rimming tyres, fixing fences, pushing 100kg blocks of lick off the semi trailer, working the cattle, branding, tagging – the lot. I was a busy bumblebee.

It wasn't always easy being the only female on the station other than the boss' wife but when the Nanny came, we had a ball! This larger than life Indigenous Australian woman honestly was a jolly friend and kindred spirit. She truly blessed me.

In the midst of the flurry, however, there were definitely times I found the bosses hard to please. I couldn't have any leftovers. I had to cook on a budget. I couldn't waste anything. It had to taste good. I could only use cheap cuts of meat (they ate the good stuff, understandably).

I could fulfil their demands but then I did it a little too well and all the workers started to gain weight... then **that** was a problem!

Come selling season, contractors arrived to help muster. It meant more mouths to feed and people from near and far arrived.

I couldn't believe my eyes.

I couldn't believe he was here.

Broughton waltzed into the station!

What a sight for sore eyes!

I didn't even know he was in the Northern Territory.

# A Sight for Sore Eyes

Seeing Broughton brought back so much that was buried.

He'd been great mates with him.

We spoke of Will, we spoke of the past, then we worked.

There was a big muster coming up – helicopters, horses, trucks and the like. We were on horseback. Things went wrong – quickly. Broughton's boss ripped into him country style. Then, so did mine.

"I'm going to f***ing bash your head in.
Get over there, you f***ing idiot.
I swear, I'll pull you off that horse and drag you under."

The abuse continued until I couldn't bear it any longer. I saw the defeat in Broughton's face. He'd had a pretty rough upbringing and definitely didn't need this.

I piped up, then it was my turn to cop it, and cop it I did until my boss in full fury fired me on the spot.

I had to finish the muster because we quite literally were in the middle of nowhere, but as soon as I was back to base, I packed up my bags and left.

During the season under the stars, I would constantly call two mentors. Janice and Cilla. Being the aged voices of wisdom that my deceased grandparents would have been, they provided sound advice and became faithful sounding boards. Nothing, however, seemed to shake the dust from inside my heart. I didn't know how to change. I didn't know where to begin. I'd listen to them and sermons, I'd soak in the Word, I'd pray. Still, nothing seemed to shift.

# The Most Unlikely Places

I was homeless. **Again**! I had no idea where to go or what to do and to make matters worse, I'd just lost my phone on the muster. Angry and overwhelmed, I drove.

I ended up in Katherine.

Ashamed and aimless, I didn't find a means to contact anyone. I wouldn't even know what to say. I didn't want any pity and I couldn't face home. I roamed the streets instead. I watched people. I tried to get lost in someone else's story but mine was deafening.

Setting up my swag in a park, Sunday was around the corner. I'd wait until then and figure out next steps.

Sunday came and after an early start walking around the Katherine Gorge, God told me to go to church in town 'Bethel.'

I arrived. There were bars on the windows. It was run down. Relieved there was not a soul in sight, I put the car in reverse and hightailed it out! There was no way I wanted to go there!

Holy Spirit said:

*Go back!*

Like Jonah, I said:

"NO!"

We argued and eventually I obeyed after He said:

*You can go somewhere else, but my blessing won't go with you.*

"FINE!"

As soon as I pulled back in, so did a bus filled with Indigenous Australian folk – right next to me.

"Heck no, Lord!"

Taken aback by my livid resistance, I was disappointed in the woman I'd become. I wasn't always racist, but there seemed to be a common thread of use and abuse with people of colour in my life.

I was supposed to spend four weeks in the lock-up ward. Twenty-eight days. They'd promised not to send me there but I understood, they needed a break.

He pushed too far. The dark psychiatrist was coloured in more ways than one.

"Now, I know you hate all these family meetings. I want to make them as easy as possible for you. Know that I am in your corner, not your family's. Can you tell me what you're comfortable with discussing today? Can we talk about x, y or z?"

**"You promised not to talk about that! How dare you, you manipulative bastard!"**

*"REBEKAH, STOP BEING SO DISRESPECTFUL!"*

"Can you not see how unstable she is? This is why we want to keep her a little longer – to see if we can help."

Spoken in a cool and collected tone, he looked at my parents with obvious concern. When my parents turned to look at me, so did he with a wicked grin.

Hot rage boiled in my veins.

28 days turned into 274.

He locked me in the cool room. I was trapped.

He pinned me to the bench. Mouth by my ear, his whispers echoed in my mind. My grip on the knife tightened.

The constant comments, the casual caresses...

The harassment had to stop. Management intervened. Their plan was to reduce my shifts from ten a fortnight to one, then in recompense they offered some *counselling*. The dark skinned chef was far more valuable than the pale skinned kitchen hand.

*"What are you doing right now? Tell me everything"*

It was after midnight, everyone was asleep.
He messaged online.

*"I want you to always be my best friend.*
*I love you"*

*"You're married!"*

Conversations with the married Pastor escalated until, horrified, I brought them into the light. We were on a mission trip in Kolkata. His blind rage and demotion thereafter nearly killed us!

Cast as a lead in a feature film, I played the country lesbian. There were a few implied sex scenes.

It was a topless photoshoot, just the Indian director and myself.

"Aww, your body is quite deformed isn't it? You don't
look very womanly at all! I'm sorry but if I keep you cast,
you'll be an offence to the gay and lesbian community.
Butch gay women often want to look more manly and,
well, you do! On the other hand... any press is good press.
When we have the radio interviews, this could actually go in
our favour and help ticket sales..."

It's safe to say, I didn't play the role.

I dare not forget the gang in South America or at times even James – the latter my supposed silver lining.

It felt like colour constantly brought pain.

How quickly did I forget the Columbian family on the coffee plantation? They literally oozed kindness. Or the Argentinian family my sister and I lived with? They took the time to teach me to cook traditional dishes. Or Eduardo, the Chilean Pastor? Then there were the Chilean locals who worked alongside the Mennonites.

I was ashamed to realise I only held onto pillars of pain, rather than the people of hope.

Another realisation hit. Why were the coloured offenders more prevalent in my mind than the white ones? Those cowboys, that family member, the directors? Completely irrational and unfair, it was my reality.

Something innately within myself needed to change.

God wanted me to go to this church. He was adamant! So, with a deep breath and nervous step, I closed my car door.

*That blessing better be upon me, Pop!*

Everyone stopped and looked.
I was the **only** 'whitey!'

It was so different to anything I could have imagined. We were already forty minutes late and instead of hurrying into the building for the service to commence, no one seemed to notice. Instead, they happily congregated on the lawn, sitting in circles under trees.

Chatting in their dialects, I honestly didn't know what I was doing. I asked to join one of the circles of women. Every now and again, a sister would graciously translate.

These women had been through **so** much. Little did I know they were in the midst of tribal wars and today was the first time people from all tribes were together in one place.

One of the women, exhausted, told her tale. The night before, some of her 'brothers' raided her house, blind drunk.

Another had been bashed.

Another had a daughter who was abused by her partner and after trying to hide at her mother's house, they all came. The men started smashing everything. Her daughter revealed herself. They took her.

### I WAS WAY OUT OF MY LEAGUE!

Finally, the doors to the church opened and with a swirling mind, we went inside. On cheap white plastic chairs we sat, then stood and sang. The haggard display folders had their local language alongside an English translation. I tried to keep up with them but gave up and silently prayed for the women I'd just met.

The preacher interrupted my inner monologue. Standing to address the congregation he said:

"I have nothing to say today. Whatever I say will cause offence to one person or another.
Can someone else please encourage us?"

No one stood up. There was silence.

JESUS, NO!

I felt the annoying niggle, then a little whisper:

> *Rebekah, I gave you a word for them at the Gorge.*
> *Go, feed my sheep.*

Standing up in the back row, I begrudgingly called out:

"I have a word for you all."

Stunned, a room full of dark faces turned to the whitey up the back. They watched in curiosity as this lone stranger made her way up to the altar.

"When I was walking through Katherine Gorge this morning, the Lord showed me these beautiful birds. They seemingly danced in the air and then would swoop down to scratch the earth. Delighted and mesmerised, I watched.

They were feeding.

God told me:

'Rebekah, my blessing and provision is all around, sometimes you just need to scratch the dirty ground. Sometimes, you need to scratch beneath the hurt, abuse, heartache and theft. Underneath the grit and grime of life is my provision – is Me. Scratch!'

Today, I want to encourage you all. I can't say that
I understand your circumstances, but what I do
understand is that God's Word is true. Yesterday, today and
forever, it is constant. So may I encourage you to scratch
past your pain and scratch past your hurt, because there you
will find God's promises. There you will find blessing and
provision – it's a promise!"

There was an altar call.
I prayed over many.

It is amazing how even in our brokenness and barrenness,
God can **still** use us.
Fruit can still be produced.

I drove whatever road I chose, never quite knowing the
destination.

I wrote.
I drove.
I wept.

Tying my swag to the boot of my car, on the side of the highway
I'd snuggle into my sleeping bag and gaze at the stars.

Longing for sleep to steal my consciousness, I'd pray.

Nothing.
Silence.

Everything seemed meaningless.

There was nowhere to go, nowhere I could escape to.
Not even in darkness.

Wanting a familiar face, dreading the concept of home,
I found myself driving to Darwin.

# Family Finds You

*Dripping with sweat, I'd arrived.*

Fear bombarded. My heart pounded. I wanted to turn and go, but where?

I had just driven ten long hours and I was exhausted!

Honestly, this was the last place I wanted to be. I didn't want to be an imposition or a burden but I didn't know where else to go.

Parking my car in the driveway, I was terrified.

Family wasn't always safe.

Unable to hold off any longer, I took a deep breath. It was time to face the music. I could see them waiting at the door. Gavin, my cousin, and his new wife Jacinta. It was too late to turn back now!

It seemed positively ridiculous! I had just driven solo across the barren countryside. I had just stood up to some rough as guts cowboys who threatened to bash a kid, not to mention spontaneously preaching at an Indigenous Australian church during tribal wars... where was that courageous woman?

I can tell you, my fear was put to shame.

Before I knew it, Gavin's strong, sturdy arms were around me.

"Bekky, it's SO good to see you."

Exhausted and battle weary, I melted into his embrace.

In that season Gavin and Jacinta were beautiful. They loved me, and then loved me some more. With grace, they gave me space when I struggled, then extended grace when I'd go to a church that wasn't always the kindest. They continually sowed into my life even though I had very little to give in return.

Their perfect love cast out my fear.

Living with them for six months, I was challenged in more ways than one. I watched how they lived, how they communicated, and I couldn't help but compare them to what James and I might have been. They, likewise, were a cross-cultural couple, but unlike James and I, seemed to make it work.

Memories of James would come and go, and with that, so too pain. Not knowing what to do with what was trapped within, a quiet niggle told me to **write**.

Overwhelmed by the concept, I didn't know where to start. Begrudgingly trying to obey, I heard:

*How did you meet?*

Flowing from memory to memory, in six months I wrote my first book *The Black and White Wedding*. Incredibly cathartic, the poison from within my heart was purged as it passionately poured from page to page.

The year was drawing to a close, as was my book. I felt an urgency to complete it before the crossover. Racing against time, with merely minutes to spare, the last words were scribed.

It was finished.

As the year ticked over, the book was finally complete, I heard the inner voice again:

*Rebekah, it's time to stop running. It's time to go back.*
*Go and face the music. Pursue your craft.*

A new journey was about to begin.

# The Train of His Robe

*"God, if this is what your people and your church are like,*
*I DON'T WANT A BAR OF IT!"*

Coming home was not an easy pill to swallow. I was unfulfilled in my job, I had to eat humble pie entering the family church, and I felt humiliated that I was living at home, again!

Pain seemed to be my most reliable friend.

Dissatisfaction reigned in my soul. I'd spend hours listening to sermons and worship. I constantly needed a touch of heaven, just a drop of living water to soothe my soul.

It was never enough. I was still in captivity.

I saw His words, I knew His claims, but where was the tangible reality of those promises? I didn't see them manifest in my life. I'd see His blessings in those I loved, His favour there, but something seemed to be constantly plugging my heavenly flow. Was it me?

Headphones in and cleaning a client's house, my favourite worship set started. The lyrics mirrored a scripture.

*The Lord, high and exalted, seated on a throne;*
*the train of his robe filled the temple.*
Isaiah 6:1

That verse **always** seemed to bug me! All I saw was a pompous God *high and exalted* with such a **huge** robe! I've walked the Vatican. I know its incredible length. I can't even fathom how stupendous the heavenly courts would be. So *this* robe's train **filled** the temple!

HECK!

The music in my ears changed. A woman stopped singing and started to explain the scripture:

*"In ancient days when Kings would battle, the winning King*
*would strip the defeated King of his robe*
*and sew it to the hem of his garment..."*

This was no ordinary robe, but a tapestry of all the victories, of all the Kings Jesus had defeated. THE KINGS!

All the ruling principalities and powers in high places, **all** were stripped of their robes – Jesus, high and exalted, was showing me:

*Bek, they're defeated! Your enemies have **been** defeated.*
*I'm wearing their robes!*

Instantly humbled, I fell to my knees. Still at a client's house, I hid in the bathroom. He truly had won the battle. Jesus was telling me I didn't need to fight anymore, I just needed to behold the victory – His victory. I needed to behold His robe.

An image of the heavens illuminated and I saw millions of people and angelic hosts straining for just a glimpse of Him and His robe. I saw the impact of such a sight. How, whenever one would see the robe, the train, they'd be reminded of the destruction of their enemies. The power and authority once ruling over them, now destroyed!

Waves of glory radiated from Him.

It was glorious!

# The Profound Presence

*The glory of His presence is profound.*
*I hear it resound.*

*There is a thick atmosphere of love,*
*it is as though I am wading in a vat of fragrant oil.*

*An incense fills the temple,*
*His temple:*
*Me.*

*The kindness of the Saviour*
*reaches near and far.*
*Encountering everyone present,*
*it is* **spectacular!**

*I had never encountered a love so rich,*
*a presence so rare.*
*The air hummed of victory*
*demolishing strongholds with flair!*

*Clothed in glory seated on High*
*was the King of Kings,*
*I let out a sigh...*

*As I beheld His majesty with awe*
*I saw such love –*
*I could not ignore,*
*all that he had done for me*
*the price he paid for liberty…*

*Lies disappeared to dust,*
*His water softened my crusty crust.*
*My heart and soul broke apart,*
*He gifted me with a brand new start.*

*He was enthroned,*
*in glory He reigns.*
*This is what His Word proclaims!*

*As I beheld the King*
*I finally understood everything.*

*Why things happened,*
*and others not.*
*In that moment*
*the pain, I forgot.*

*It was never about any success,*
*joy, laughter or even distress,*
*but solely about a loving King –*
*encountering and finally worshipping Him!*

# The Light Within

Darkness fell over me. I was home. Walking into the house that hummed with history, I felt it all. It was scribed in its bones.

I could hold off all day, I could keep temptation at bay, but as soon as I walked across that threshold, a hollowness came.

Emptiness would gnaw, light would be swallowed up by darkness. I would hear its call, its taunts and haunts until I'd finally heed and obey.

I would become prey.
In the midnight hours.
I'd hide.
I'd binge.
I'd purge.
I'd lie.
Trapped.

Desperation bombarded. A fear rose as I fell deeper into darkness' grasp. I opened the fridge, the cupboards, and the drawers. I knew in an instant I could make a banquet for one. I also knew the repercussions. A shower, the guilt thereafter, the state thereafter...

I had to make another choice.

It had been months now, every day I would fail. Every day, I would fall into the pressures of my mind. I would allow the fear, the turbulence within to dictate my choices. I would turn to food and then attempt to rid my body of it. I would continuously sabotage and ruin the gift God had graciously given me – my temple, His temple, my voice.

Eating and purging into the wee hours of the morning, darkness had me in its grasp. Hidden in the confines of my solitude, I would allow its power to reside and take over. Lust would flare like a flame. My eyes I could no longer tame as I'd devour images and movies that would feed the beast of the night. I was trapped. The cycle would continue, day after day, night after night.

I'd leave the house with a painted face. I would put on the façade but inside I was full of lard. I was dead within. The pain was palpable. I knew not why. What instigated this? What gave it power to reside?

Me.

Something needed to change.

I needed to change.

Yes, the revelation was common sense, common knowledge, but no matter how hard I'd try or what I'd try, the cycle seemed to continue. Something would trigger the beast, lure it out... when it was out, that was it.

Whenever I'd come home, the beast would say 'hello.' A knowing feeling would overwhelm me. The fight would begin. Darkness would plague.

I didn't understand how I could be under such a stronghold, especially when my parents loved the Lord and sought after Him – so did I. Where was this foothold?

It only takes one light to illuminate darkness.

Beyond being frustrated, I knew the principle. Light and dark cannot coexist... so why did it happen here?

The voices were loud. The feeling is intense. I didn't want to succumb, but what was my defence?

Jesus.

He had **just** told me to look at Him, to behold Him, to dwell on Him.

I cried out, then opened the fridge, the cupboards, the doors – but this time, I closed them.

This time, when I called out, He answered. This time, when I cried, He heard my plea.

Opening His word, not knowing where to turn, the answer came to me.

*Your eye is the lamp of your body.*
*When your eyes are good, your whole body is full of light.*
Luke 11.34

I had fed the cycle of darkness. It wasn't just with food, it was likewise with my sight. I gave the voice power. I gave the thoughts ammunition by dwelling on them, meditating on them, fighting them. By doing that I remained in their clutches.

*What I empower contains **the** power.*

I needed to follow Helen Lemmel's advice:

"Turn your eyes upon Jesus, look full in His wonderful face, so the things of earth will grow strangely dim in the light of His glory and grace."

I needed to look at Him. Dwell in His presence. See the robe.

I needed to feed the light and bask in it because darkness couldn't remain.

Darkness wouldn't remain in Him.

# Enraptured and Captured

I saw her post.

She was positively breathtaking – effortlessly so.

Successful. Striking. Sexy.

Her reflection in the elevator doors was mesmerising. Stilettos, trench coat and a trace of lace modest enough for you to take a second glance, alluring enough to be imprinted on your mind. She stood there. Breakfast in one hand, phone in the other. A few strands of hair escaped the soft bun, her face was framed perfectly by the lenses she wore. I looked and was in awe!

How did she always seem to look just right?

A part of me, an unsightly part of me, reared its head.

*You could never be that beautiful.*

What an encouraging inner monologue!

The thing was I positively adored this woman. I couldn't care less if she was wearing sweatpants and a hoodie, or a silk ballgown – it was the essence of who she was, the woman inside the clothes. That's who I adored.

I merely coveted the rest!

How often when I looked at my own reflection, did I hate the woman I saw? Not the clothes, not the appearance, but the woman?

A deep sadness washed over me.
I didn't love myself and didn't know where to start.

It would be simple enough to take an 'in' frock and use it as a shield, hiding behind the garment, the façade. But how often would I comply with society just to feel a sense of belonging? Validation?

Too many.

*You can't lead when you fit in,*
*because then you're being led!*

It was time to discover who Rebekah Anne Mowbray truly was, and it was time to finally **love** her!

# Spiritual Awakening

Trying to find a new normal, I settled back into my old job – caring for the aged and disabled. I went straight into forging a path in the entertainment industry and made an effort to get an agent, return to acting classes and hone my skills.

It turned out that Pop had some plans of his own! Every single acting class, he would give me a word of insight or encouragement for each woman in the class – **every week**!

There was one actress to tick off that list and, by Jove, I did **not** want to! For three weeks, Pop nagged and nudged me through the entire class.

I can be stubborn!

Finally, we were working together. Helping her with her lines, I held her phone. It was locked and her home screen illuminated the music she'd been listening to...

Hillsong.
Wait... she's *Christian*?

"Okay Pop, I'll give her the word."

*Coward.*

175

Turns out, the word of encouragement and insight I gave her was an answer to a prayer she'd been praying for weeks. Her response from God could have come a whole lot sooner if I'd just obeyed.

Sorry, Dani!

I asked if she'd found a **good** church. Now I was **very** weary of church, to say the least, and even though she believed she had found one, I didn't believe her. I told her I'd check it out, just to make sure it was alright for her. I didn't want her to be hurt like I'd been and for some strange reason, I felt ridiculously protective of her. I needed to keep her safe!

God truly works in mysterious ways.

Little did I know that in the delivery of that word, a door of destiny would open for me. I was about to visit Glow.

# The Four Walls

Arriving at Glow Church – ironically held at Eternity Theatre – I was instantly not impressed. Everyone seemed fake, fake, fake! The music wasn't to my taste. Their smiles were too big. I didn't believe them for a second! They all dressed too modern and to be quite frank, I was not having a bar of it!

> I tried not being **so** obvious to Dani...
> if I'm honest, I was pretty transparent.

In worship, I glanced over at Dani. She was literally **lit up** like a Christmas Tree.

> *Man, I didn't want to dash her heart*
> *but still...*
> *I wasn't buying it.*
> *She could get SO hurt by these people.*
> *These... hypocrites.*

Who would have known how much dirt had seeped in my heart, into my soul? Who knew how poisoned I'd become by church?

Definitely not me.

Utterly relieved when church had finished and I'd said goodbye, I was positively **mortified** when I heard Pop tell me to go **back** the following week!

"WHAT?"

God definitely had his work cut out. Not only was I on an emotional journey of wholeness but somehow now, to my utter horror and dismay, I'd found myself pushed onto a spiritual journey of restoration as well...

GREAT!

No wonder He tells us to walk by faith and not by sight.
If I had foreseen this, there was **no** way I would have given
Dani that word!

# Kicking and Screaming

My journey at Glow was definitely love-hate. At first, I literally went there kicking and screaming – in spirit and just a touch in reality.

In my arrogance, I didn't hold back from telling the worship Pastor what I thought about the worship culture. I may have touched on what he could improve and perhaps implied I could give him a few pointers...

As I write, I shake my head in mortification.

Who was I to say such things? How could I possibly know his true capacity when we'd only **just** met?

The fact is, I didn't. All I heard were songs I was triggered by. All I saw were lights, a *show*. All the while, all I truly felt was the pain of the people in my past who'd had his role and failed. I was coming from a springboard of pain which inhibited my sight to see the gift on his life and what God was doing in the church.

My past was not the best platform to cast judgement.

*Judge not lest ye be judged...*
Matthew 7:1

I met a connect group leader, Amy. On a roll and in full bulldozer style, I told her each and every detail that needed 'work' at Glow.

> Who would have known she'd become *my* connect
> group leader?

When I first saw this proper Pommy princess flitting here and there in her heels, she quickly caught my eye. She was a woman who knew her value and unashamedly walked in it.

I liked her immediately.

> Amy had this uncanny ability to see the unseen, to reach
> people on the fringe and draw them in – even if they were
> as distasteful as myself.

I watched as another connect group leader crossed her path, Roma. I saw their exchange. Jealousy reared its ugly head!

It was quite extraordinary as we'd only just met. I couldn't believe I was jealous but what I saw in their exchange, I wanted in on. When I saw the genuine love in their eyes, all I thought was *Cat*. I thought of all that had been lost and I pined for the past. Within that exchange, quite extraordinarily, I saw hope in the now and in tomorrow.

With a silent plea, I prayed:

> "Lord, I want to be Amy's sister. I want her to love me like
> one – like she loves Roma. And, jeez, can it **not** take a year?
> I don't want to wait that long. Yes, I do realise it will mean
> I'll probably have to stay at this church. Bugger. But I'll do
> whatever I need to... just let her love me."

Interesting how desperate for love I was from these
so-called *fake* people.

Annoyed that Amy had to run off to do a church errand – and
ridiculously put out that she'd connected me with Roma –
I was very disconcerted. Not only was I jealous of Roma, but
Roma was the most stunning Indian woman I'd ever met. I was
intimidated by her on so many counts. She had the complete
**opposite** personality from me and I had **no** idea how to talk
to her. She appeared to be very content with silence. Silence
made me want to SCREAM! My thoughts would get louder and
they'd race faster.

Amidst my loud inner monologue, I sensed I was seated next
to someone extraordinary. Deep down, I really wanted to get
to know her and become her friend. But I had no idea how to
connect with her.

Again I prayed:

> "God, would you do a miracle and help us become friends?
> Good friends please, Lord. **Really** good friends – like her
> and Amy? If I'm honest, I don't think it's possible since I
> am speechless and **so** uncomfortable around her. But Lord,
> help me. Show me how."

He did.

Time at Glow church changed my life.

Pastor Grant Hoyle was very different from other pastors I'd
encountered. Young, tough, tattooed and raw he was a man of
gumption, a man of his word.

When I saw him, I knew he wasn't afraid to speak the truth. I knew he would fight for the lost, for the unseen – for that I instantly respected him. Even though I didn't trust other men that walked those halls, I did trust him.

With time my perspective changed.

I changed.

Extraordinarily within a year, both Amy and Roma became my sisters. Both captured my heart and although many internal battles still raged, I'd finally found a home at Glow, and later a housemate in Roma.

# She was Lifeless

B inges were every day. Purging as well. But now I faced a problem – the plumbing could not withstand the demand. A smell seeped into the house.

I needed another method of attack.

In such an utter state of defeat, I was getting more and more complacent in my secrecy. I may have found a church, but I was still bound!

I took the bucket and the bag into the living room.

Nearly one in the morning – the lights were out.

In full purging swing, my worst nightmare played itself out.

Mum walked in.

I tried to hide the bag of 'mess.' She kept coming.

Horrified, I begged her to stop. I told her what I was doing. I tried to clean it up.

"PLEASE don't see me like this... please Mum, stay away."

She stood by the brick archway and near the lounge chair. I saw the look of horrified pain in her eyes, then she fell...

In slow motion, I watched her fall.

She crumpled.
Her head hit the sofa.
She started convulsing.

I screamed.

Running to her weeping, I held her in my arms as I bellowed:

"NO, GOD!"

Her body eventually stopped shaking. It was now lifeless.

Rocking her in my arms, tears cascaded down my face.

I screamed:

"NO, MUMMA. DON'T LEAVE ME. DON'T GO. MUMMA,
I'M SO SORRY.
I'LL CHANGE. MUM, COME BACK TO ME.

**GOD HELP ME!**"

I didn't know what to do.

I just held her body and rocked.

My delicate, fragile mum.

She came to and was completely unaware of her surroundings or what happened – everything.

She found herself in my tear-drenched arms and then she started screaming:

"YOU'RE OKAY. Rebekah, you're going to be fine!"

Jumping up, full of adrenaline, she started running in circles.

I forced her to stop and sit before she passed out again.

I bolted to the other end of the house. I needed to wake up Dad.

Now it was my voice and body that shook.

Dad became a rock. He did what needed doing.

They went to the emergency room.

Alone in the house, sobbing once more, I vowed I would change.

I would never let that happen again!

# In the Deadlock

I was in a church I loved. I was surrounded by beautiful people. But when all would go to sleep, when all would be in bed, night would still come.

This stronghold still had such a grip on me.

The week before, I'd snuck out with the bucket and bag, I'd climbed out my window. Silently and deceitfully, I crept into the bushland across the road. I drove to find a deserted car park... all for the sake of relieving myself. Ridding my body of all.

Embarrassing, to say the least, it was the truth.

It had never been this bad.

Then Mum. The doctors had no explanation. She just *fainted*. I knew that was not the case. I felt life leave her. I saw the blank expression of lifelessness. It completely horrified me.

Something had to change quickly.

I reached out to my now mentor and friend Amy, a weeping, seeping mess. She listened and got down to business.

"What's the plan?"

"Flip, Ames, how the heck am I supposed to know?
I've tried EVERYTHING! All I know is I can't stay like this
much longer. I'm drowning. I want to give up. I won't.
I can't – man, I don't know."

"What's Pop telling you?"

"If I'm honest, I can hardly hear him now...
It's like He's gone silent.
Ames, I feel like a ticking time bomb, like I'm in the lock of
death – physically, mentally, spiritually.
I don't know how to get free."

Amy would pray. What a woman of gold. Thereafter we decided, we'd fight this together.

Monday became our fasting day.

*I cannot let it win – but the victory is beyond my view.*
*With the little strength I have left, Lord,*
*I leave it in your hands.*
*With the little faith left in me, I pick up your shield.*
*With the rest of the courage I possess, I stand.*
*I **will** stand on your promises.*
*I will not hide anymore, but I will look at my shame, my pain,*
*and my dysfunction.*
*I will stand in the middle of my storm.*
*There, I will call out to the King of Kings and Lord of Lords.*
*Chained, lashed, bruised and abused, I will look into the light.*
*I choose to see only the light.*

*In the midst of my chains, I will be transformed by Your light.*
*Another chapter will commence.*
*I have to believe it will.*
*Lord, I choose to dare greatly in you.*
*In YOU I choose to stand.*

# Who's Blaming Who

Even though we fasted, even though we prayed, victory did not come. I understood that the neural pathways had been forged over nearly two decades, now a seventeen-year battle with an eating disorder. Thereafter an addiction to porn, not to mention twenty-two years battling depression and mental health.

Still, I wanted a 'quick fix.'

The Monday Fast Day was now inclusive of another connect group leader, Fiona. I knew I was not alone. Those women became absolute pillars, but it was relentless. The storm continually raged.

Dawn had come. I didn't wake early enough. I was sprung!

There was a bustle in the kitchen and deep-seated dread filled my being. I'd failed yet again.

If it wasn't enough that last night was such a disaster, this morning I didn't have enough time to replenish the 'stores.' Exhausted beyond comprehension, I didn't want to exist. I wished the day away.

Work called.

It was enough for my family to know the disaster I was, for Amy too, but I couldn't let anyone else see.

Quickly and efficiently, I got up and tried to wash away the shame. It did very little. When I walked into the kitchen, Mum's face said it all.

A butter knife could have cut through the silence.

I left without a word, shame heavy in my heart.

I cried out to God, I wanted the pain to depart.

In my desperate cry, a story came to mind.

It was the story of Adam and Eve.

The story had fast-forwarded and commenced when Eve became deceived and ate the apple. Adam, by his wife, knowingly ate as well.

Playing out as though on a movie screen, I watched as momentary satisfaction transformed into monumental despair. I watched despair fill their spirits as they saw their nakedness for the first time. I watched as they desperately went to find something to cover their shame.

A fig leaf.

I saw the fear in their eyes when they heard the sound of the Father walking in the stillness of the afternoon. It was the same fear I felt at dawn. Pure and utter desperation. They would be discovered. I was discovered.

God said:

"Adam, where are you?"

He didn't call Eve, who was deceived, but Adam who knowingly ate the apple. Like me.

In Adam's fear, he **blamed** Eve and she then blamed the deceiver. But God was talking to Adam, not to Eve.

As I sat in my car, dreading the clients I would have to serve that day, the soft conviction of the Spirit nudged at my heart. Angry, I went to blame Mum and Dad. I went to blame the abuser. I went to blame the bullies at school. I blamed the sickening addictions I was bound by. I went to blame, **blame, blame**. I didn't want to acknowledge that I had a part to play in my shame.

God said:

*Bek, you know I've promised to strip your sins as far as the east is from the west. I have likewise done that for your Mum, your Dad, the abusers, the bullies, your oppressors. As far as the east is from the west.*
**Gone!**
*When I see them, I don't see their past sins, nor yours, I merely see the slip-up of the moment.*
*Stop using those past instances as leverage for the enemy.*
*Take off those glasses, look through my eyes.*
*Look at me.*
*Look at them through me.*

Convicted, I repented. I had bound my family and the people of my past to account for the pain they'd caused. I had much to learn on forgiveness.

Then God said:

*Rebekah, you need to look at yourself the same way. Forgive yourself. Wipe away the memory of your sins, as far as the east is from the west.*

*See yourself as the glorious daughter you are.*

# I Involuntarily Shook

Frantic, I started to pace. Agitation like a stubborn itch was trying to steal my now and my tomorrow. I tried to slow the racing, but it became manic. The feeling was manic, not my thoughts.

Then, they joined in...

Fear took a hold.

"I can't stay this way. I can't go down this path again. Freedom is right in front of me. I can't give in. I can't give up."

An opportunity arose, I wanted to bolt.

Why?

It's the most ridiculous thing, the most ridiculous response to a blessing – re-enacting a curse!

It made me think...

"Am I cursed?"

"Why is it that I cannot seem to break away from this barrage within?"

The cupboards were opened, then closed. Contents emptied. The routine continued. I forced myself to stop – to call a friend.

They didn't answer.

I started to sweat.

Voices. I heard the voices now.

Louder. LOUDER.

I wanted to scream, I wanted to weep at once. Instead, I saw myself edging back into the kitchen.

**No!** Too much evidence would be left.

*Find an excuse. Go into town, buy the binge, then discard the contents in the bush. You'll feel so much better!*

"God, I can't follow that voice. I can't heed to that song!"

An email popped up. A book was waiting for me at the library

*YOU HAVE YOUR EXCUSE. GO!*

**"Jesus, HELP me!"**

The itch intensified. I couldn't run from it. The only way it would go away was to scratch it. But I knew the scratch led to death. I knew that!

I was just so tired. So exhausted after another sleepless night, I didn't want to withstand another internal fight. I could just do a *little* binge. No one would be the wiser. My face wouldn't swell too much...

I'd have to be quick – I knew how.

Collecting my handbag, I went to my room with the intention of retrieving a reserved library book. But there, sitting on my bed was the book. Graciously, Mum had picked it up.

I wanted to scream! I no longer had a valid excuse to go to town, and I didn't want to lie when I knew they'd ask. A white lie is one thing, but an outright lie is crossing a 'Bek line!'

### **"JESUS!"**

Grabbing both books, I left.

I opened the front door and a sadness I cannot express enveloped me.

I didn't want this to be my story.

"Jesus, I don't want to live this way."

I tried another friend.

They didn't answer.

Internally, voices were screaming. Externally, my body started to shake.

I had never experienced withdrawals like this. A racing mind, sweat dripping from my brow, my body literally rattled. I thought withdrawals this severe were only for drug addicts? I'd never seen this side of the fight.

A thought came to mind.

*How long have you **really** committed yourself to fighting? REALLY fighting?*

OHH, GOD! Am I an addict?

*Write it.*

"God, what good will that do?"

*WRITE IT!*

"What do I say?"

*Say you are writing 'from victory, into victory.' That you are more than a conqueror. That you deserve this role, no matter how small it is. Write that you **are** a new creation.*

Right now in this moment, as I walk through the front door, I am declaring that I **am** a new creation. I **am** more than a conqueror. I **am** beautifully and wonderfully made. I **am** worthy of love and success. I **am** victorious.

# Deafening Defeat

When you don't think you can continue, how do you?

*I didn't know how to do it,*
*I didn't know how to change.*
*I didn't want to do it,*
*my life rearrange.*

*I knew I was not alone,*
*there were people by my side.*
*But I didn't want them to see*
*the truth behind the lie!*

*I didn't want them to face*
*this mighty battle with me.*
*The mess, the trauma, the loss –*
*my reality.*

*Every time I'd sit to write*
*a guilt would plague my mind.*
*I'd fallen off the wagon,*
*I was still caught in its bind!*

*Once again, I didn't know*
*what I should do.*
*I knew I had to continue,*
*to start the moment new.*

*Despair would start to reign,*
*would this always be the case?*
*Would I ever escape this nightmare?*
*Would I ever win the race?*

*Then I heard His voice:*

I'm transforming you into glory,
each and every day.
It's a journey, my daughter,
I have made a way!

You are not alone,
I promise you'll see the end.
You will reach the summit,
you'll get past this bend!

I have hand-picked your family,
I know your destiny.
They are power-filled and relentless,
determined to see you free!

Their tenacity of spirit
was specifically chosen for you,
to walk you into victory –
your dreams will come true.

This freedom is not just yours
but for generations to come.
The sacrifice they have made
was for everyone!

The harvest will be plentiful,
it's waiting there for you.
It's time to reap all you've sown –
Rebekah, start anew.

Do not give up, do not give in,
for if you stay and win the fight
your legacy therein will begin.
Day will dawn from night!

With **every** problem, I will provide a promise and provision.

FIND IT.

HOLD ONTO IT.

DO NOT RELENT.

# The Joy of the Lord

I always heard the scripture:

> *The Joy of the Lord is your strength.*
> Nehemiah 8:10

I just didn't understand how to have that 'joy.' How do you tap into that happiness?

I'd watch other believers, I'd see their plastered smiles and all I'd think was "*hypocrite!*"

I couldn't talk or say much because, lo and behold, it was exactly what I was doing! I was sick of my repetitive response to the traditional 'Christian greeting' of:

*"How are you?"*

\*Cue fake smile\*

"I'm struggling, but okay... always get there in the end."

I was sick of constantly seeing their forced smiles in response. I was sick of being the manifestation of that hypocrisy! My life very clearly didn't reflect the blessings that God promised and nothing had changed. Week in and week out, it seemed to be the same. How the heck was I supposed to tap into the 'joy' the Bible spoke about?

I know it says consistently to renew the mind, but was that it? That I needed to have *happy* thoughts?

A scripture came to mind.

> *Rejoice in the Lord always, again, I say rejoice...*
> Philippians 4:4

Well, what if I didn't want to...

> *Rejoice always, pray continually,*
> *give thanks in ALL circumstances.*
> 1 Thessalonians 5:17

Rebekah...

> *Let everything that has breath, praise the Lord.*
> Psalms 150:6

> What was it about praise and worship?

I didn't feel like singing. I didn't feel very grateful or like professing His goodness... look where I was again!

> That's when it hit me,
> the revelation hit me.

The world tells us to rejoice when we're joyful, when we're happy, but the Kingdom tells us to rejoice in **all** seasons! It is in the rejoicing that we tap into the joy of the Creator... **that** was how I would find another key to breakthrough.

> Glorify His name!
> That's how I could win the battle!
> 'Re' - peating the 'joy' – singing!
> Rejoice.

As with King Jehoshaphat, worship needed to be at the forefront of the battle. The singers needed to rejoice on the frontline so the sound of worship could rattle the enemy, causing them to turn on themselves and self-destruct. Like with Saul and Silas, when they worshipped in prison, chains loosened and prison doors opened.

It was time to fight like the ancient warriors!

*I am Alpha and Omega, the beginning and the end, the same yesterday, today and forever.*
Revelations 22:13

Perhaps His principles and war tactics were timeless too?

It made sense that there was such resistance to singing – to proclaim His goodness and worship His name. It was in worship that my mind would be transformed, that I would no longer fixate on my mountains or enemies – I would have dove eyes upon my King. It was in praise that I would no longer dwell on my pain or loneliness, but I would find comfort in the presence of the Almighty comforter. It was in thanksgiving that joy would well, hope would swell, and strength too.

It was all in the song. All in the sacrifice of praise.

That was the key to freedom.

That was my sword for success.

Now, I just had to wield it.

# Ancient Battle

*It has begun.*
*An ancient battle rages.*
*The sound of the shofar resounds.*
*Feet pound on the muddy ground.*
*The clanging of metal deafens.*
*It is the cry of war.*
*Blood, sweat, life carpets the earth.*
*What was, is no more.*
*It is finished.*

Pop told me to fight like the ancient warriors –
I didn't know how.
He told me to rise above the storm –
I was too weak.
He told me to remain within the Eye,
the Eye I had to seek.

Where was it?
How could I remain...?
There was so much to train within me.

*In the stillness*
*then,*
*He showed me*
*the battle already won.*

*I just needed to abide,*
*spend time solely with the Son.*

*As I did abide,*
*the victory I did see.*
*I found then I was empowered*
*to walk in His glory.*

*The beauty of His presence*
*made me want to sing.*
*That in essence destroyed*
*every binding thing.*

# The Uncomfortable Truth

*It was confronting, uncomfortable.*
*It was **TRUTH**.*

Sitting in church, the leaders in training were in training.

*My strength is made perfect in your weakness.*
2 Corinthians 12:9

Really, *God?! They're **really** going to preach on this?*

The sermonette was a siren of conviction after conviction, and was exactly what God had been talking to me about too.

### What did I do with my weakness?

They dipped into 'excuses.' They highlighted 'responsibility in circumstances.'

*Are they honestly going to preach about 'the consequence of choice' now?*

I was not a fan of the preach but, honestly, it was true!

I did need to 'stop asking for a way out,' and rather ask for a way through! That is what this book is about – the retraining of my psyche to successfully make it to the other side. Going from victory **to** victory.

2 Corinthians started to murmur in my mind:

> *My strength is made perfect in your weakness...*
> 12:8

God's strength? Honestly, the scripture made me more and more frustrated. For years I had been weak, for **years** I'd fought and called out to Him... why hadn't I seen the manifestation of His strength? Had I just been too blind to see, or was it never truly there?

The sermon continued.

> "Partner with what He's doing."

What on earth did they think I was doing? Twiddling my thumbs? I'd sacrificed what seemed like **so** much of my life, my dreams and my desires to try align myself to Him, to be prepared. But what good did that do? Other than bring up a whole load of issues I'd really have preferred to remain dormant!

> *You are not a victim or weak, Rebekah. I gave you my Holy Spirit. It's inside you and I am by your side.*

> "Pop, can you stop with the commentary, please?"

> *When you start acting like the powerful daughter you are, when you start owning the power I gave you, then yes. Absolutely!*

"Geez, that will **never** happen!"

*It definitely won't when you keep that attitude up!*

The silent banter continued until the next point in the sermon.

I felt another shock wave.

"Stop seeing spiritual leaders as enemies."

WOW!

It was like all the scum at the bottom of my spirit became stirred. Images of leader after leader started to flash through my mind. It was a 'then and now' scenario. I saw them when they hurt or betrayed my trust, and then saw the favour of the Lord upon their lives now.

It made me mad.

I felt taunted once again, that I'd wasted **so** much of my life harbouring this silent pain. I may have hidden it from sight but I didn't realise how much residence it took up in my inner man.

I started to lick my wounds.
Would life ever be fair?
Would I ever be able to fully trust
church leaders again because,
honestly, they'd been more like enemies?

THEN IT HIT ME.

If the enemy of my soul could convince me that all church leaders were either going to let me down or abandon me, there'd be no way I'd consciously or subconsciously partner with them. Why would I give them the position to speak into my life, if they'd only hurt me after?

I knew I was part of a bigger picture in my church, but if I couldn't get over my offence, I would never be an asset. In fact, I'd be a liability.

I needed to forgive.

Just as I thought I was well and truly done, I was once more hit by the preacher.

"STAY IN YOUR LANE.

If the enemy can keep you doing 'good things,'
but not 'God ordained things,' he'll have won. Distraction will have stopped you from attaining your full God-given potential.
Three degrees misaligned will result in a **very** different destination 100kms down the lane."

I didn't want that.

"God, don't ever let that become my reality. Please, Jesus!
Teach me to remain where you've called me."

*Then trust. Stand on my truth, listen to my voice and trust me.*

# The Chafing of Conviction

*I am a spiritual being,*
*a fact I've known since a child.*

Always intuitive, always able to sense and absorb the spiritual climate, I learnt it was a gift especially when cultivated correctly. However, when it's not it becomes a hindrance.

Recently, Pop revealed just how undisciplined I'd been with that treasure.

I would allow myself to be influenced by my surroundings and inner battles. I would surrender my power to cultivate the future I desired by meditating on the waves of the world, on the turbulence within. I had seemingly allowed the temperature of my mind, and that of the environment I was in, to govern my inner life. I was not being the thermostat nor the cultivator of life I desired.

Admittedly, I would push aside love as I'd allow an atmosphere of fear to take a hold. I would push aside favour by dwelling in an atmosphere of lack, and I would push aside fruit by dwelling in a state of fruitlessness.

I ignorantly empowered my current circumstances to remain, rather than cultivating the crop I desired.

Pop had already told me:

*Whatever is true, noble, right, pure, lovely, and admirable, think about such things.*
Philippians 4:8

Likewise, He said to:

*Put off my old self, which was being corrupted by its deceitful desires; be made new in the attitude of my mind.*
Ephesians 4:23–24

He kept going.

*Do not conform to the patterns of this world but be transformed by the renewing of my mind.*
Romans 12:2

He was trying to get through my thick brain that it wasn't His responsibility but **my** responsibility to cultivate an inner life of goodness and favour. It was up to **me** to train my mind. It was up to **me** to pull out the weeds and the lies, and it was up to me to sow seeds of truth until transformation eventuated.

Whatever I'd cultivate within would bear fruit without.
That was a promise!

In saying all that, a realisation struck.

It was my choice how I wanted to steward my inner garden.
It is my choice what I want to grow.
The choice is **mine** about what sort of life I want to have!

I may not be able to control all circumstances that come my way, but He has granted me both the power and the authority to choose how to respond to them. I have the power to cultivate an inner life of success.

Jesus warned me:

*The thief comes only to steal and kill and destroy; I have come that you may have life and have it to the full.*
John 10:10

Then it hit me... I didn't really know what a 'full life' looked like.

A quiet whisper beckoned.

*Pull out the weeds. You'll find out.*

It was time to let go of the lies and to see them as they truly were. It was finally time to take a hold of the truth – to see and eat its cultivated fruit.

I would claim the promise.

I would walk in and out of that promise.

Finally, I would claim the victory and I would become victorious!

# The Knock of Guilt

*Guilt is knocking*
*Do I let it in?*
*NO!*
*I have wiped **every** remnant of sin!*

*No guilt or condemnation comes from above –*
*only the truth,*
*purity and love.*

*You **are** an overcomer,*
*today and forevermore.*
*Fly on wings like eagles,*
*above the storm – soar!*

*Do not look at what was,*
*only at what I show thee.*
*Bask in victorious glory,*
*hold on to liberty!*

*Listen not to all those lies,*
*see them for what they are.*
*Listen to my truth,*
*then you will go FAR.*

*My child, trust in Me,*
*I'll show you what to do.*
*Then you will see,*
*My promises come true!*

# Will it to Stay or Go

*Whatever you have, has permission.*

L ike it or not, God in His graciousness has given us all free will. He gave me a choice.

> *I lay before you life and death,* **choose** *life.*
> Deuteronomy 30:15

I certainly did not choose my circumstances, but I have held the power to choose what I do with them.

I chose how I respond.

It's a challenging concept that within choice lies accountability. I don't like that! They say ignorance is bliss but honestly ignorance is exactly that – **IGNORANCE!**

I believe bliss is the satisfaction of acknowledging an issue and taking responsibility for it. It's choosing to put a stake in the ground and using whatever means possible to change your reality. Bliss is when reality has shift. Bliss is the realisation that you **are** a conqueror, for you **have** conquered!

When I tried to grab hold of that concept, guilt would knock on my door.

"How many years have you suffered?"
"How many years have you made *others* suffer?"

I couldn't keep that mindset.
I knew its destination.
Death!

I won't pretend there aren't principalities and powers, demonic strongholds and influences, however, Satan is the 'king deceiver.' Had I been deceived into believing the lie that I was more bound than I was? Had I in fact been chaining myself?

Was I deceived into believing that the *powers* which governed my choices were stronger than Almighty God?

In all honesty, *yes*.

The battle has been brutal. The strongholds **strong**. But, had I known my own strength would that have shift the focus of the battle? If I'd known how to proficiently wield the sword and against whom, would chains have loosened quicker or easier?

In my life I appear to have stayed rooted in a position of ignorance, pain and powerlessness for quite some time. Had I known my true power – and had the required endurance I'm positive I wouldn't have had to withstand the fight for so long.

If within my life there has been no fruit, if within my life there has been a stronghold, I believe it remained because I did not shed light on it. It remained because I knowingly or unknowingly allowed it to stay.

This concept has been hard to grasp. I've battled for **years**. I tried with my own sheer strength until I exhausted myself and all those around me. I used 'worldly ways' and self-help principles to combat spiritual encounters and knock on doors of the unseen.

A common thread in it all was...

I HAVE TRIED.

How could I forget that what lies within me is the **fullness** of wisdom, knowledge and understanding?

How could I forget that I merely needed to tune into the heavenly radio station within me to hear *that* still, small voice?

My key to freedom was to be found in stillness and pruning was to be performed in the stationary.

Equipping was provided in the quiet.

# Tuned In

I was still on the carousel and frustrated.

Nothing had shifted.

"God, I don't understand.
How is it that I can pray for others – watch as they receive their
breakthrough – yet my life is still an image of warfare?
I'm tired and although I won't give up, I'm at a complete
loss about what to do!"

*Did you research how ancient warriors fought?*

"No... but I know you told me to."

*Do you want your answer?*

With the search bar open before me, I Googled 'Ancient
Biblical Battles.'

I sat and I read.

Text seemed to hum. An answer was here, I knew it.

223

*The Israelites were being delivered from slavery.*

I definitely **felt** like a slave!

*Moses delivered them from the Egyptians...*
*He led them into victory through the parted Red Sea...*

Then the Spirit stopped me.

*Rebekah, I have not called you to be delivered instantly like*
*the Israelite slaves,*
*I called you to be a servant deliverer like Moses.*
*The higher mantle calls for a higher price.*
*Are you willing to pay it?*

**Wow.**

For years I had longed to see His manifest power in my life. I had longed for Him to instantly break decades of debris, however, He wanted to cultivate something greater within me – the chain breaker anointing. God wanted to develop capacity within me so I could lead people into freedom like Moses.

That mantle carried a price. Was *I* willing to pay it?

"Pop, I don't know how to live up to that higher calling.
I don't know how to carry that mantle."

*Trust me. I do!*

*I didn't tell Moses everything ahead of time – if I had he'd never have done it – but if you stand side by side with me and continue to abide, you will do things you never dreamed possible.*

*I will complete the good work I started within you.*
*I promise.*

# The Ancient Presence

*An overwhelming sadness overcomes me.*
*I can't escape it,*
*I can't outdate it.*
*The ancient presence remains.*

*There is a dread I cannot compel*
*to stop, to leave – to not dispel*
*all its remnants on me.*

*Too late,*
*it's done.*
*Drowning in its sea.*

*I'm gasping for air.*
*I'm gasping to breathe.*
*My throat constricts,*
*I start to choke.*

*Sight turns blurry and grey.*
*This will be my very last day.*
*My mind like a carousel*
*round and round, I want to repel*
*all that is within me...*

*Faster.*
*Faster we spin*
*until*
*darkness.*
*An abyss.*

*Trapped in a world*
*where death and life kiss.*

*Alone.*
*Afraid.*
*Not knowing who's the maker*
*and who is made.*

*On the tightrope of reality –*
*one missed step*
*and victory.*
*For, I am not sure who,*
*me or the voice –*
*the keeper or the zoo?*

*Do I step and carry on*
*or jump off and see*
*what lays among*
*the dark and empty space?*
*I'm ready to end this constant chase.*
*The choice no longer mine to make,*
*the rope frays and then it starts to break...*

*Gone.*

*Falling in an abyss of darkness*
*between space and time,*
*I wasn't quite in reality –*
*I hadn't reached divine.*

*I was nowhere,*
*I was somewhere.*

*Not knowing what to do*
*there was nothing for me to hold on,*
*then within my spirit*
*resounded a powerful song.*

*It was Mum's voice.*

*She was singing over me.*

*Breath came into my lungs.*

*I gasped –*
*light.*

*Light invaded the abyss.*
*And time.*
*I heard the ticking of life.*

*Opening my eyes,*
*held in her embrace*
*I was home.*

# Home

As though a prodigal, I returned home. Daunted and haunted, it was time to finally fight and face the beasts that taunted me and my family for generations.

It was time to reclaim stolen ground.

During the journey of reclamation I saw the truth of my parents. I realised their response to my eating habits and mental state were never founded on disappointment or shame, rather rooted in fear and sadness. I now saw their pain for what it was – **love**. It stemmed from an inability to take away the burdens I carried.

I saw a generational line of sexual abuse, mental illness and addiction – alcohol, drugs, porn and food. I saw spiritual strongholds and with that renewed sight too.

Daily, my parents and I started praying over the family.

Our relationship began to significantly shift.

During that season I realised when I eventually have a family of my own, I want my family to be safe. The next generation needs to be different and for that to take place, the beast needs to be defeated in this generation!

In my heart of hearts, I know we hold victory. I have seen transformation in my sisters, in myself and in the family. I know the journey will continue, but hope and truth are now my anchors – not disappointment and defeat.

I know the love of my God, my Father. I have come to recognise His kindness and see how He's ever so subtly guided my footsteps. I've come to recognise that I was never forsaken in my valley of darkness – a friend or a light was always there. At times it felt like it was hidden, however, it was always close in my time of need.

He always answered my prayers. It may not have been in the way I expected, but in hindsight He always delivered.

The church I now find myself in is one of those answered desires. The people I initially judged so harshly are now family. I truly love them all.

Merely a few months after attending Glow I surprisingly found myself registering for 'GLP,' the Glow Leadership Program. It was a free twelve month course designed to instill practical leadership skills in those who felt a call of people leadership in their life – inside and outside the church. Who would have thought I'd find myself in a position of speaking life into others' lives?

To carry any position of influence, I felt in my innermost being that I first had to change! If I were to speak into someone's life, I needed the authority and victory to do so.

There was SO much pain, so much challenge – everywhere.

As I spoke to different women within the church and heard stories of despair, I realised even though some tales were similar to mine, in my current state of defeat I was nothing but a sounding board. I didn't carry the weight of breakthrough in my spirit nor house the authority to release it.

That needed to change.

I began to fight but learnt I couldn't fight alone – I was never destined to fight the battle alone. None of us are.

There is a reason God calls us His army...
an army stands and fights as one.

I had to position myself within the community; be vulnerable, real and also malleable to change.

# Posture Changes Everything

Amidst a community of Christ's believers, I was challenged to contribute, trust and also combat the ideologies I previously held against 'their kind.' Wanting to avoid the heartache of my past, I battled between a desire to erect a sturdy barricade around my heart and the prompt to build a bridge.

I knew what I had to do.

Slowly but surely, I built a bridge with my choices. Every choice to be seen, heard or known became another rung towards restoration.

I started to see breakthroughs, significant breakthroughs. I postured my ear to hear. I postured my heart to feel safe enough to break, but also to be restored.

I finally saw God as our conductor, leading and guiding His orchestra. I had a community that was gracious enough to be patient with me – to listen, forgive and truly journey with me. As I did the same, our lives became the most beautiful symphony.

I made myself malleable. I was willing to do the internal work and they were willing to stand in the gap. Side by side we fought each other's battles, we also played together.

Now as I look to my left and right, I see a progression of victory in all of our lives.

It takes courage and trust on everyone's part,
but most of all it takes one **very** gracious and
loving God to make music from us all.

*Seek and ye shall find.*
Matthew 7:7

# The Unseen

As I was unpacking boxes a hidden life became visible. There were letters and cards, from people in my past wishing James and I well – wishing me well. They were people I remembered from a lens of pain rather than love – the reminder now in my hands.

Tears dampened my cheeks.

I read letters one by one and remembered, differently. Taken aback I realised I'd held onto memories of pain. Now, I saw through a different lens. I walked the path of pain and had been crushed by it. Now it was new wine, new truth – I remembered the love.

Somehow in the chaos of the storm, I forgot love. I forgot the kindness I'd been shown by people in that enchanted village. My memories had been so distorted by darkness. I'd singularly held onto pain. How many friendships were lost? Too many.

The trajectory of pain is blinding, deafening – it's paralysing!

The more I sifted through boxes, the more hidden blessings I found. There were trinkets, letters and gifts from people who'd been pillars of empowerment and love in a season. Prized and preserved, they'd since been forgotten.

I realised I couldn't take for granted these pillars in my life anymore. I could not forget them – it was now time to honour them. Time to honour those past and present who still stood strong.

In my hands was a card from Janice, my singing teacher. It seemed like a lifetime ago. In my adolescence she helped piece together both my voice and my heart. She still is a pillar of power and more like a grandmother. Over the years she has challenged, inspired and empowered me to be the best I can be.

Initially demonstrated through tough love, Janice was a representation of her teachings, and her mindset. I always found myself inspired by Janice. I admired the woman. More loyal than man's best friend, she has become family over the years. Following my travels with emails, calls and messages, she has been a faithful light – one I truly treasure.

Cards from Havalah and Kathryn fell on my lap. These two women were friends before the abuse and they are still friends today. They've seen me at my best and my worst. They've weathered the test of time and the test of distance. In my hands lay that reminder.

Love and gratitude welled within my soul. It appears I never truly was alone.

In the sobering moments of unpacking my past, I saw the kindness of God. He had positioned pillars of love in my life in every season. They may have been scattered around the world, they may have been pillars unseen, but they all stood by me through thick and thin. They were bedrocks.

Today, I thank God for each and every one of them. His hands and feet were continually outworked through them – they still are today.

# The Eye of the Storm

*In the midst of a storm,*
*I was encompassed by love.*
*It was to my undoing.*

*The walls of protection,*
*the walls of fear*
*were sturdy and fully erect.*
*I was ready for battle.*

*Armed and ready for attack*
*I braced for the oncoming...*

*Then I saw those eyes.*
*They looked into mine*
*and I into them.*

*With not one ounce of shame,*
*with not one speck of condemnation,*
*with not an inch of disappointment*
*I melted in the sight of love.*

*There was pain,*
*but not from shame.*
*It was shared, it was mine.*

*As I peered into the window of the soul*
*the image was one of shackled anguish.*
*For they had no power or ability to change my circumstance*
*or my outcome.*

*Not knowing what to do,*
*I saw their pure intentions.*
*It was the first time I had allowed myself to feel*
*those pure intentions –*
*to touch them*
*and embrace them.*
*To see them:*

*Love.*

*For too long I mistook the look.*
*For too long I wore the lens.*
*For too long I judged.*
*I blamed.*
*I condemned.*
*It was not the other way round.*

*Out of the fear of attack, I attacked.*
*Out of the fear of judgement, I judged.*
*Out of the fear of condemnation, I condemned.*

*Out of shame.*
*Out of guilt.*
*Out of pain.*

*Finally, I saw.*
*Finally, I knew that I was not alone.*
*But we were in the Eye of the Storm.*

# The Impassable Path

During a counselling session nearly a decade ago, the Christian counsellor prophesied that I'd write a book about 'from freedom into freedom.' She believed I would glean keys to victory and write about the journey. From that she prophesied that breakthrough and hope would manifest for many. Struggling with her word of insight and encouragement, I tossed it aside. I'd attempted to find the keys but deep in my pit, I was blind. I wrote a few pages and a few points, but eventually gave up.

Now, in my hands is that lost notebook. I remember her words today as clear as the day she'd released them. I read the points I'd scribbled down back then in obedience. I feel both the longing and despair of that season.

Melting into the moment, holding that tattered notebook, today I feel the love of God. He did fulfil His promise. I would write a book. Incredibly, the first point scribed so many years ago is now the last point I feel to write today.

Sleep, far and in-between, rarely gave rest.

Disoriented, I woke up startled. Another nightmare. I was exhausted.

Fighting to orientate myself, a sadness settled in.

I still hadn't changed.

I seemed to battle the same enemies time and time again. I had relentlessly exhausted each and every method of attack – still defeated.

A voice rose from within my soul:

*What if you weren't meant to fight this battle?*

Baffled, I didn't understand. Of **course** I had to fight this battle. I cringed at the notion of surrendering to it.

*Rebekah, sometimes I place impassable obstacles in your path to **stop** you from following through! I know where the path is leading you, I've destined you for greater. You need roadblocks to force you to look up at Me so I can show you another way. You need to stop focusing within...*

More than ten years ago, this was the first point I scribbled down in that tattered old notebook:

*Look up, not in.*

I have since learnt sometimes God places impassable obstacles in our path to elevate us. He forced me to look up to Him so he could raise me up to higher levels – so I can reach a different destination.

I'd been fighting an ancient battle on a carousel. Nothing was changing. I kept going round and round on a stationary steed.

The battle was won on the cross, yet I couldn't seem to appropriate that victory. I was still seated on my stationary horse. Little did I know, a stallion was waiting. I just needed to jump off the carousel to ride it.

God didn't want me to continue struggling and fighting the same battles day after day, year after year. He wanted to elevate me so I would see the battle as won, so I could start a new journey with the dawning sun.

During a church fast, slowly but surely, in His kindness He started to elevate my thinking and posture of position.

Days had passed, I hadn't fallen off the wagon. My body felt different. Triggers came, but as I looked up to the King, as I locked myself away the urges passed.

I stood firm and withdrawals came and went.

I realised this would be an ongoing journey of abiding and residing. But, no longer was I fighting from my previous vantage point. I'd finally learnt to hide in His presence.

Now on a different path, my eyes were fixed on my King. I knew we would be victorious one day, one moment at a time. We would walk into that promised land and so would many others.

Setting aside that musty old notebook, I thanked God with reverence.

He truly does script the end from the beginning.

*I am Alpha and Omega, the first and the last,*
*the beginning and the end.*
Revelations 22:13

# The Shattered Reflection

*When I looked in the mirror I did not see beauty,*
*but the brutality of my past.*
*When I looked in the mirror I did not see softness,*
*only hardness of heart.*
*When I looked in the mirror I did not see a future,*
*I only saw the past.*
*When I looked in the mirror I saw what was hidden*
*behind the crafted mask.*

*He smashed it.*
*The mirror,*
*right in front of my eyes.*

You are not what you see.
You, my child, radiate with beauty.
My beloved daughter,
Princess of the King –
you can conquer **everything.**
When you fight,
you are **not** alone.
I am with you,
the Ultimate capstone.
Look not at what was,
only what is to come.
Wear your royal robe –
*a new journey has begun.*

# FROM THE AUTHOR

*T*he Shattered Façade is about walking 'into freedom from freedom.'

It was initially titled *More than a Conqueror* but the Spirit had other ideas.

Two years ago, I started this project but didn't get far. I wrote a total of 5 mini-sermons before giving up. I was far from truly free and writing about freedom seemed hypocritical.

On the 12th of December 2020 I felt God tell me to pick up the project and finish it by the end of the year. I thought it was an impossible task – I had barely written any of it!

Then I heard Him say:
"Write the context. Write your story so the weight of your revelations will be revealed."

That day I sat and wrote.

From 5am to 10:30pm *The Shattered Façade* was penned. The 5 sermons slotted in beautifully, poetry poured forth to compliment the tales, and before I knew it a broad stroked painting of my life was script on paper.

The book was complete! Well, the first draft.

During the writing process I was confronted with the fact I fought heaviness for years and simultaneously ran from it.

Intimidated, I was terrified of the pain of my past and did everything in my power to avoid it.

I nearly destroyed myself in the process.

I have had to go on a journey of **facing** my storms, facing my pain – the guilt, my shame. I had to face my past and stay in that uncomfortable space, all drenched, cold and wet, until the storms eventually passed.

Then I was blessed with a rainbow, a promise and a victory.

I pray this book becomes the encouragement you need to do the same. You can face your storms courageously.

You are not alone, you can obtain victory irrespective of what anyone has said or done to you.

It's time to *shatter the façade*.

It's time to unashamedly '**be**' who you were created to be.

*Take courage.*
*Ride the storm.*
*Welcome the warrior.*
*Meet the victor in hiding.*
*Become the conqueror within.*

# ACKNOWLEDGEMENTS

First and foremost, I must give honour where honour is due: to my God. In my darkest hours you never left me. So kindly and delicately you took my ashes and made them beautiful. Thank you. Thank you Jesus for loving me in my wretchedness, and in turn teaching me to love myself out of it. I would not be here if it was not for the knowledge, revelation and encounter of your steadfast nature.

To my family. You have loved me when I knew not how. Words fail to relay the depths and heights we've journeyed together, and words fail to communicate the gratitude and love I have for you all.

Mum and Dad, you have sacrificed more than I care to share. You have cultivated a spirit of tenacity and determination in all of us girls, and for that I will always be grateful. The sleepless nights, the constant prayer and those morning bush walks will never be forgotten.

Pilot Naomi and Doctor Sarah, I could not be prouder of you both. You love and support so differently, but when push comes to shove, you have both fought for and with me. I am so grateful to call you my sisters, to have you in my corner, and be able to do the same for you. Thank you for choosing to love daily when you could have very easily chosen differently.

Roma Christian, without your support this book wouldn't be. You are a visionary, a woman of action and the most faithful friend. Thank you for introducing me to my publisher, Jane. Thank you for going above and beyond time and time again. You have nudged me to continue, you have whispered words of destiny, and you have been by my side every step of this 'book journey.' The gratitude I have for you runs very deep in my heart. Whenever I see this book, I will forever be reminded of your generosity and see your fingerprints on it.

To my publisher Jane Turner, thank you for caring so deeply. You have gone out of your way to support and iron-out the little creases in this publishing journey. What a journey it has been! Thank you so much for supporting me until the very end.

To my graphic designer Samantha Nagle and photographer Kate Williams, thank you. Sam, your artistic skill and attention to detail is honestly beautiful. Thank you for the time, love and effort you've poured into both the book design and myself.

Thank you to all the booksellers, my readers and most importantly, thank you God.

May this scripted testimony be a seed and a legacy of freedom for many.

Milton Keynes UK
Ingram Content Group UK Ltd.
UKHW010855040923
428018UK00004B/435